HOME REPAIR AND IMPROVEMENT

FIREPLACES AND WOOD STOVES

TIME®
LIFE
BOOKS

OTHER PUBLICATIONS:

DO IT YOURSELF
The Time-Life Complete Gardener
Home Repair and Improvement
The Art of Woodworking
Fix It Yourself

COOKING
Weight Watchers® Smart Choice Recipe Collection
Great Taste/Low Fat
Williams-Sonoma Kitchen Library

HISTORY
The American Story
Voices of the Civil War
The American Indians
Lost Civilizations
Mysteries of the Unknown
Time Frame
The Civil War
Cultural Atlas

TIME-LIFE KIDS
Family Time Bible Stories
Library of First Questions and Answers
A Child's First Library of Learning
I Love Math
Nature Company Discoveries
Understanding Science & Nature

SCIENCE/NATURE
Voyage Through the Universe

For information on and a full description
of any of the Time-Life Books series listed above,
please call 1-800-621-7026 or write:

Reader Information
Time-Life Customer Service
P.O. Box C-32068
Richmond Virginia 23261-2068

HOME REPAIR AND IMPROVEMENT

FIREPLACES AND WOOD STOVES

BY THE EDITORS OF TIME-LIFE BOOKS, ALEXANDRIA, VIRGINIA

The Consultants
Stephen Bushway, a mason specializing in
building masonry heaters and chimneys, is also
a certified chimney sweep. The inventor and
manufacturer of Ultimate Ridgehooks, he
operates Deer Hill Enterprises in Cummington,
Massachusetts. He is the author of *The New
Woodburner's Handbook* and writes for several trade publications. Mr. Bushway currently
serves on the Hearth Products Association
Solid Fuel Advisory Committee to the Massachusetts State Board of Building Regulations
and Standards. He is also president of the
Massachusetts Chimney Sweep Guild.

Richard Day spent eight years with the
Portland Cement Association as a writer and
editor on subjects relating to concrete and
masonry. He has designed and built a number
of fireplaces from the ground up. Based in
southern California, he has written numerous
articles for *Popular Science* and has authored
several books on concrete and masonry.

CONTENTS

Improving Fireplaces and Wood Stoves

A roaring fire in a fireplace has a voracious appetite for both air and wood, but it can also devour heat. By drawing warm air from the rest of the house, a fire can actually raise heating bills. But you can make fireplaces and wood stoves more efficient by performing some simple measures such as installing glass doors, adding a chimney cap, extending the flue, and puttting in ceiling fans and registers to improve air circulation.

Sealing a crack in a wood stove →

Heating a House with a Wood Fire

Heating a house with wood is more involved than simply stoking up a fireplace or installing a wood stove. To be safe and efficient, wood-heat appliances must be wisely situated and installed to current building-code standards. Understanding how heat is distributed will start you on the road to setting up the heating system that best suits your needs.

Heat Distribution: Wood-heat appliances such as stoves and fireplaces distribute heat through a house by convection, in which heat travels through moving air. Although this process occurs naturally, it can be boosted with fans *(opposite)*.

Some houses are better suited to wood heat than others. A New England saltbox, for example, can be heated efficiently with one central-ized heater. The heat will naturally rise by convection to warm the rooms upstairs. A sprawling ranch house, however, would require a system of fans to move the air—or additional heaters. A well-insulated home of any design will also be easier to heat than one that lets warmed inside air escape and cold outside air seep in.

Other factors affecting heating efficiency are the placement and length of the chimney or stovepipe. The best location is the center of a house, where the flue—the channel that passes exhaust from the appliance up through the roof—stays warmer, promoting convection of heat from the flue. Also, the taller the chimney, the longer the column of warm air inside and the stronger the pull, or draft, which feeds air to the fire. A chimney that is too tall, how-ever, may not draw well if the air inside cools before it reaches the top.

Efficient Heaters: To burn cleanly, a fire needs sufficient oxygen *(below)*. An open fireplace draws far more air than it needs for combustion. It sends this air, along with much of the heat produced by the fire, up the chimney. Thus, a fireplace's heating efficiency, or the amount of the wood's potential heat transferred into usable heat, is extremely low—10 percent or less. Modern fireplace designs are some-what more efficient *(page 10)*, but no fireplace can match the performance of a well-designed wood stove *(pages 11 and 33-35)*. Ideal for heating a large area—or an entire house—a good wood stove burns as cleanly as possible and maximizes the amount of heat it produces.

WATER VAPOR

The three stages of combustion.

In the first stage of a fire, water in the wood evapo-rates. The heat from a kindling fire or coals raises the temperature of the logs and essentially boils away the water they contain. The drier the wood, the shorter this phase. As the temperature of the wood rises, it begins to vaporize into the combustible gas-es and tar droplets that make up smoke *(above, left)*. If the temperature in the appliance is high enough and there is enough oxygen, the smoke will burn, producing bright orange flames *(above, center)*. Unburned smoke forms creosote, an air pollutant. In well-designed appliances, the fire enters the char-coal phase once most of the gases and tar are gone. The red glow of a charcoal fire produces very little smoke or flame *(above, right)*. As logs are added to an ongoing fire, all three phases can occur at the same time in different parts of the appliance.

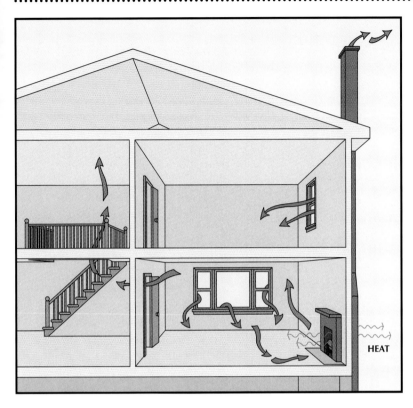

The chilling effects of a fireplace.

Much of the warm air produced by a fireplace, indicated by the orange arrows at left, can actually be wasted. As the fire burns, the air it needs for combustion is drawn from elsewhere in the house and from the outdoors through gaps around doors and windows *(blue arrows)*, creating cold drafts. When the air entering the fireplace is warmed, it rises up the chimney, carrying much of the fire's heat with it. At the same time, the heat radiated by the fire itself warms the air in front of the hearth, but if the chimney is located on an exterior wall, heat will also radiate outside. Meanwhile, the warm air in the room rises and pools against the ceiling, leaving a layer of cooler air below. At the door the warm air escapes and travels up the stairwell, where it pools on the upstairs hall ceiling. There it is blocked from upstairs rooms by the wall above the upstairs door, even with the door open.

HEAT

A system that minimizes heat loss.

When the heat source—in the case at right, a wood stove—is located in the center of the house near the stairwell, most of the heat produced by the stove is circulated indoors *(orange arrows)*. Weather stripping on doors and windows blocks cold air from the outside, eliminating one source of drafts. To improve the dispersal of heat through this house, part of a wall on the ground floor was removed. A ceiling fan *(page 28)*, which can also be used for cooling in summer, spins at a slow speed, forcing down the warm air that collects at the ceiling. Wall and floor registers *(page 29)* help warm the upstairs rooms: The wall register above the door allows the heated air in the stairwell to enter the room even when the door is shut. The floor register, near a corner of the room, allows warm air from the ground floor to rise by convection when the ceiling fan is off. When the fan is on, the floor register acts as a return vent for air set in motion and circulated through the house by the fan.

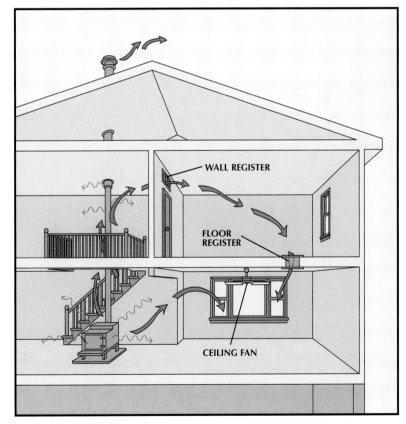

WALL REGISTER

FLOOR REGISTER

CEILING FAN

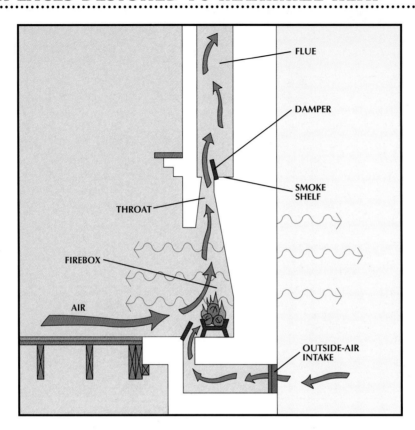

A fireplace that fights heat loss.

This design—known as a Rumford—is the optimal one for an open fireplace. The wide, shallow firebox radiates heat back into the room, boosting heating efficiency as high as 15 to 18 percent. An air intake underneath the firebox draws outdoor air into the fire through a hinged opening on the floor of the firebox, lessening the amount of warm air drawn from the room and up the chimney. The air feeds the fire, then rises up the tapered firebox throat past the damper into the flue. The damper can be adjusted to enlarge or reduce the size of the opening into the flue, thus regulating the suction, or draft, created by the air that fans the fire. When the fireplace is not being used, the damper can be closed entirely to prevent cold air from entering the room.

A cavity that generates heat.

A circulating fireplace draws in cold air through a floor-level vent and heats it in a space around the firebox, expelling the warmed air through vents at the top. Most circulating fireplaces have glass doors. Their value is twofold—they reduce the amount of air flowing up the chimney and contain heat in the firebox to warm the air flowing around it. The air needed for combustion passes through a damper at the base of the doors, providing enough air for a good draft but siphoning less room heat outdoors. While this design is a significant improvement over an open fireplace, fireplace inserts are even more efficient (pages 35 and 43-45).

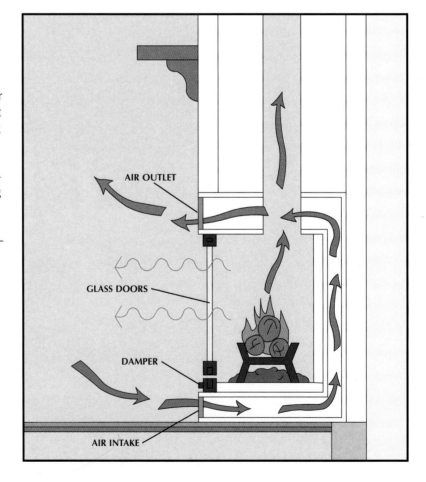

THE MECHANICS OF THE DRAFT

How draft is created and perpetuated.

When a fire ignites, smoke, exhaust gases, and hot air from the firebox rise past the open damper into the smoke chamber. From there they follow a spiraling upward path, gradually warming and reversing cold downdrafts from the mouth of the chimney; simultaneously, the fire begins to draw air into the firebox from the room; and the pattern of the draft is created. If the draft is too weak, the fire will smolder; if it is too strong, the fire will burn too quickly. Good draft depends on a number of factors. The flue must be correctly sized in relation to the firebox; a flue or firebox that is too large or small will hinder draft. Likewise, draft will slow in a flue that is too short or long. A flue's shape and inside surface are also important. Spiraling smoke rises more easily in a cylindrical form. In square or rectangular flues, smoke eddies and collects in the corners, slowing airflow *(inset)*. Similarly, a flue thickly coated with soot or creosote, or one whose sections are connected with rough mortar joints, will disrupt the flow.

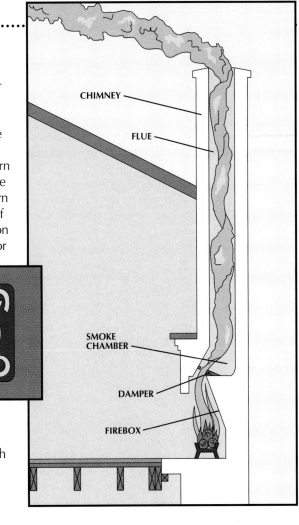

CHIMNEY

FLUE

SMOKE CHAMBER

DAMPER

FIREBOX

A STOVE ENGINEERED FOR EFFICIENCY

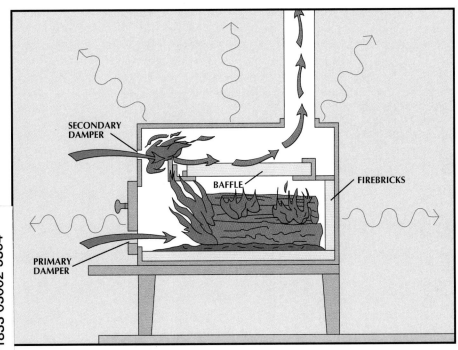

SECONDARY DAMPER

BAFFLE

FIREBRICKS

PRIMARY DAMPER

A practical heater.

The wood-burning stove at left is loaded from the front through a tight-fitting door equipped with two dampers. The primary damper supplies air for combustion; the secondary damper provides air for ignition of the volatile gases released by the burning wood. Extending from the back of the stove, the baffle forces these rising gases to the front where, fed by air from the secondary damper, they ignite. The result is more complete combustion of both the wood and gases than in an open fireplace. The firebricks lining the sides and bottom absorb the fire's heat and release it slowly, even after the fire has died.

Whenever a fire is lit in a house, it should be treated with great respect. There are three immediate hazards associated with a fireplace or wood stove: The fire may escape directly, in the form of hot embers or sparks; its radiant heat may be great enough to ignite nearby combustible materials; or flammable residues in the chimney may catch fire and spread to adjacent wood framing or to the roof.

Preventing Fire: You can virtually eliminate these dangers by installing and operating a wood-burning appliance with care, inspecting it regularly, and keeping it in good working order. When putting in a system, observe national and local building and fire codes as well as the manufacturer's installation instructions. Keep hot embers from escaping an appliance by installing glass or metal doors. An open fireplace should have a metal mesh screen or glass doors, and andirons or a cradle-shaped grate to keep burning logs from falling or rolling beyond the firebox opening. Transport ashes in a covered metal container.

Chimney fires occur when creosote buildup on the inside of the chimney gets hot enough to ignite. The best prevention is to operate a clean-burning appliance *(pages 32-35)*. Also, inspect the chimney often and clean it as necessary *(page 111-115)*.

Smoke Detectors: Powered by either battery or AC current with battery backup, these devices are available in two basic designs—ionization and photoelectric detectors. Each is best suited to different areas of a house *(opposite)*. Test all smoke detectors once a month and clean them occasionally to keep dust from reducing their sensitivity.

In Case of Fire: Establish escape routes from every room of your home, using ground-floor exits and emergency ladders from upper floors, and make sure all members of the household are familiar with them. Include a meeting point outside so you can confirm that everyone has exited safely.

Keep an ABC-rated fire extinguisher near the door of any room that contains a wood stove or fireplace. Familiarize yourself with its use so you can put out a small fire. For a large fire, or any fire you cannot contain, the safest response is to leave the house immediately and call the fire department from a neighbor's home.

SMALL DEVICE THAT SAVES LIVES

Installed much like a smoke detector *(opposite)*, a carbon monoxide (CO) detector *(below)* can alert you to the presence of this lethal gas. Normally consumed by the fire or expelled via the chimney, CO may seep into the house if the stove malfunctions. The device should be placed at least 15 feet away from the fire source, preferably in the center of an adjacent room. Don't locate a CO detector near a ceiling fan, since the fan will disperse the gas before the detector can sense it.

CARBON MONOXIDE DETECTOR WITH SILENCER

Locating detectors.

There are two types of smoke detectors: ionization and photoelectric. Ionization detectors respond quickly to smoke from clean-burning fires of paper and wood; however, they tend to sound false alarms if placed near a fireplace or wood stove. A photoelectric detector is more appropriate for areas adjacent to any room with a fireplace or wood stove. Install ionization detectors elsewhere in the house. If a staircase is open, mount one near the top. If the stairway has a door, place one near the ceiling of the room below since the dead air in the stairway may prevent smoke from reaching the device. Wherever possible, mount a smoke detector on the ceiling in the center of a hallway or room. Avoid placing them in dead-air spaces at the corners of a room, and install at least one on each floor of the house.

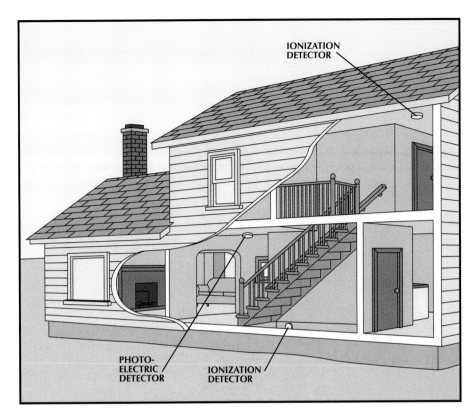

IONIZATION DETECTOR

PHOTO-ELECTRIC DETECTOR

IONIZATION DETECTOR

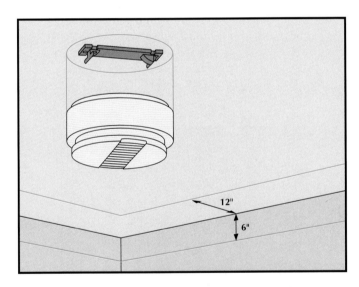

12"

6"

Situating a smoke detector.

Position a ceiling-mounted detector at least 12 inches from the wall, and a wall-mounted unit at least 6 inches below the ceiling. In a room with a sloping ceiling, place the device about 12 inches below the highest point, where smoke tends to pool. If the ceiling has exposed beams, mount the detector on the bottom of a beam, not in the space between beams.

KEEPING A CHIMNEY FIRE FROM SPREADING

Easily identified by its thunderous roar, a chimney fire can be particularly dangerous—in an old or poorly maintained flue, flames can spread invisibly to the house's framing. The best course of action is to leave the house and call the fire department. However, if you catch the fire within a few minutes after it starts, you may be able to contain it.

For a fireplace, stand about 6 feet from the firebox with your back to an exit, and douse the fire with an extinguisher; sweep it back and forth, coating the logs from the bottom up. Once the fireplace is out, close the damper to cut off air. With a stove-flue fire, close all the air vents on the appliance to starve the fire of oxygen. With either a stove or fireplace, keep the damper or vents closed for at least 30 minutes to prevent the fire from reigniting. Outside, hose down the roof with water, but avoid spraying the chimney—it may crack.

The efficiency of a fireplace depends largely on the proper functioning of the firebox. Problems generally result from either structural damage or flaws in the design. Fortunately, many of these defects can be easily remedied.

Improving Airflow: Poor air intake can cause a fire to smolder and die. Check for a faulty damper *(below)*; if the damper is in good working order, you can alleviate the problem by supplying a source of outside air *(opposite)*. A smoky fireplace is often due to faulty draft—the airflow up the chimney is not strong enough to pull up all the smoke. Install glass doors to regulate airflow and reduce the loss of heated air up the chimney *(opposite)*. Decreasing the size of the firebox opening with a smoke guard can help *(page 16)*; or you can increase the draft by extending the chimney *(pages 20-21)*.

Refurbishing the Firebox: Crumbling mortar joints in the firebox are easy to fix *(page 17)*. If the damper frame breaks, consult a chimney professional—the frame is usually anchored in the masonry. Or, you can substitute a top-sealing damper *(pages 19-20)*. To help prevent future damage, keep the weather out with a chimney cap *(page 19)*. Poor design can be partially offset with a fireback—a decorative cast-iron plate mounted on the back wall of the firebox to absorb heat and radiate it into the room.

 TOOLS

Wire brush	Wrench	Ball-peen
Pliers	Electric drill	hammer
Screwdriver	Masonry bit	Caulking
Putty knife	Cold chisel	gun

 MATERIALS

Lead anchors	Fireplace
Smoke guard	mortar
Glass fireplace	cartridge
doors	

 SAFETY TIPS

When using an electric drill or chipping out mortar, wear safety goggles. Add a dust mask when cleaning soot from the damper.

MAINTAINING A DAMPER

Variations on a common design.
The damper controls the size of the opening between the firebox and the smoke chamber *(right)*. Some dampers have three movable parts —the damper plate, a ratcheting arm, and a handle *(left inset)*. With others, only two parts move: the plate and a ratcheted handle *(right inset)*.

With a powerful flashlight, check whether the plate is out of its track. If so, take it out by removing the cotter pins or bracket bolt, and clean debris and soot from the damper-frame groove with a wire brush. If necessary, use a soot-cleaning product.

When you cannot return the damper plate to its track, install a top-sealing damper *(pages 19-20)*, or consult a chimney professional.

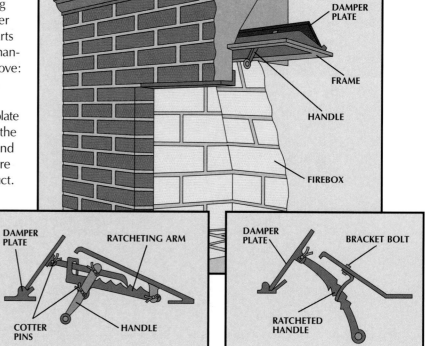

SMOKE CHAMBER
DAMPER PLATE
FRAME
HANDLE
FIREBOX

DAMPER PLATE
RATCHETING ARM
COTTER PINS
HANDLE

DAMPER PLATE
BRACKET BOLT
RATCHETED HANDLE

IMPROVING THE DRAFT WITH GLASS DOORS

MOUNTING BRACKET

LINTEL CLAMP

INSULATION

1. Positioning the frame.
◆ Attach the mounting brackets and lintel clamps to the glass door frame with the screws provided.
◆ Holding the frame at an angle *(left)*, slip the lintel clamps under the lintel—the metal or masonry beam that supports the bricks above the firebox opening.
◆ Push the bottom of the frame into position so the top and sides are flat against the face of the fireplace, making sure the frame is centered over the firebox opening. Push any protruding fiberglass insulation back behind the edges of the frame with a putty knife.

2. Anchoring the frame.
◆ If the frame has bottom brackets, drill holes for lead anchors in the floor of the firebox with a masonry bit. Insert the anchors and fasten the brackets to the anchors with the screws provided.
◆ At the top of the frame, slide the lintel clamps against the lintel, then use a wrench to tighten the pressure bolts against the lintel.

LINTEL

PRESSURE BOLT

AN OUTSIDE VENT TO BOOST DRAFT

In a well-insulated, tightly sealed home, a fire can be starved for air. One simple solution is to install an outside air vent, available as a kit from a fireplace specialist. A floor register is installed within 3 feet of the fireplace and connects to an air inlet on the outside of the house by means of a flexible hose running under the floor.

REDUCING THE SIZE OF THE FIREBOX OPENING

ALUMINUM FOIL

1. Establishing the lintel height.

◆ Tape a sheet of aluminum foil across the fireplace just above the lintel so the sheet overhangs the firebox opening by about 4 inches *(above)*.

◆ Light a small smoky fire in the firebox —one fed by newspaper or dry leaves.

◆ If smoke still enters the room, tape another sheet of foil across the opening about 4 inches below the first. Repeat, if necessary, until smoke no longer spills into the room.

◆ Leave the foil in place during several fires to check the adjustment.

SMOKE GUARD

2. Installing a smoke guard.

◆ Buy a smoke guard sized to match the combined width of the foil strips taped to the fireplace in Step 1. Choose a spring-loaded model you can custom-fit to the width of your firebox opening.

◆ Compress the smoke guard against one side of the opening, then release it slowly *(left)*, making sure that its top edge fits tightly against the lintel.

REPAIRING FIREBRICK MORTAR JOINTS

1. Applying fresh mortar.
◆ Chip away any damaged mortar with a cold chisel and ball-peen hammer.
◆ Clean soot and debris from the damaged joints with a wire brush.
◆ Dampen the joints and surrounding area with a wet rag.
◆ Using a caulking gun loaded with a cartridge of fireplace mortar, fill the damaged joints *(right)*.

2. Smoothing the mortar.
◆ With a putty knife, smooth the mortar flush with the surrounding firebricks *(left)*. Scrape excess mortar from the bricks.
◆ Let the mortar cure for 24 hours before lighting a fire. The first fire will darken the new mortar to match the color of the old.

Work at the Top: Rejuvenating a Chimney

Inspect your chimney annually for obstructions. Before lighting the first fire of the season, open the damper and shine a strong flashlight up the flue. If you see any obstructions, clean the chimney *(pages 111-115)*. A chimney cover *(opposite)* will help keep debris out. Also clean and adjust the damper *(page 14)*. If it is broken or cannot be adjusted properly, you can install a top-sealing damper *(pages 19-20)*.

Extending the Chimney: When a fireplace lets smoke drift into the house, it is because the draft is poor *(page 11)*. A well-designed chimney extends at least 3 feet above the point where it passes through the roof, and rises at least 2 feet above the next-highest structure within 10 feet, such as a dormer or tree. If yours does not meet these criteria, you can extend it with terra-cotta flue liners and bricks *(pages 20-21)*.

The chimney's crown may not be properly beveled so as to direct air currents upward over the flue. A crown can be reshaped or rebuilt with mortar as you would when extending the chimney.

Sealing Smoke Leaks: Leaking smoke anywhere along the length of the chimney is a serious problem; it signals cracks in the masonry—a potential fire hazard. If you suspect your chimney is leaking, perform this simple test: Cover the top of the chimney with a towel, then place a smoke bomb or a smoky flare—available at fireplace supply stores—on the smoke shelf and close the damper. Examine the exterior of the chimney for smoke—from outside, and inside on each floor and in the attic. If smoke is seeping through, do not use the fireplace until you remedy the problem. For an unlined chimney, install a stainless-steel flue liner *(pages 22-24)*. If the chimney has a terra-cotta liner, the leak may be the result of structural damage or deteriorating mortar joints in the liner. Since the repair may involve tearing down the chimney's outer wall, consult a professional.

 TOOLS

Wrench
Wire brush
Electric drill
Masonry bit
Ball-peen hammer

Screwdriver
Wire cutters
Cold chisel
Caulking gun
Handsaw
Hammer
Mason's trowel

 MATERIALS

Chimney cover
Top-sealing damper
Fireplace mortar cartridge
Terra-cotta flue liners
Bricks

Mortar ingredients
  (Portland cement,
  hydrated lime,
  masonry sand)
2 x 6s
Common nails (3")
Plastic sheeting

 SAFETY TIPS

Wear goggles and gloves when mixing, applying, or chipping out mortar. On the roof, don nonslip rubber-soled shoes.

SAFETY AT HEIGHTS

Safe practices are essential whenever you work on ladders or roofs. You can rent, purchase, or build equipment to help you move around securely, but your personal tolerance for heights should be the determining factor. If you don't feel comfortable off the ground, have the job done by a professional.

When you use a ladder, make sure it is level; place its feet on a board, if necessary. Lean an extension ladder against the house so the distance between its foot and the wall is one-quarter the distance it extends up the wall. Never prop a ladder against a window or door; keep it away from electric lines, and add a stabilizer to keep it from slipping sideways. When you climb the steps, don't carry anything in your hands—wear a belt for tools and supplies. Never stand above the second-highest rung of a stepladder or the third-highest rung of an extension ladder.

If your roof slopes less than 4 vertical inches for every 12 horizontal inches, you can generally move around on it with no special safety apparatus other than nonslip shoes. For a pitch greater than that, use safety equipment intended for steep roofs. Create footholds with ladder hooks *(page 41, Step 6)*. For added stability, set up scaffolding *(page 61)*. Use ridge hooks *(right)* to secure roof scaffolding in place or nail it to rafters.

PROTECTING A FLUE WITH A CHIMNEY COVER

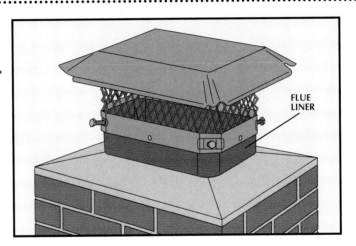

Securing a chimney cover.

◆ Buy a prefabricated chimney cover to fit the size and shape of your flue liner.

◆ Slip the base of the cover over the top of the flue liner, then tighten the bolts against the liner to hold the cover in place, as shown at right.

FLUE LINER

INSTALLING A TOP-SEALING DAMPER

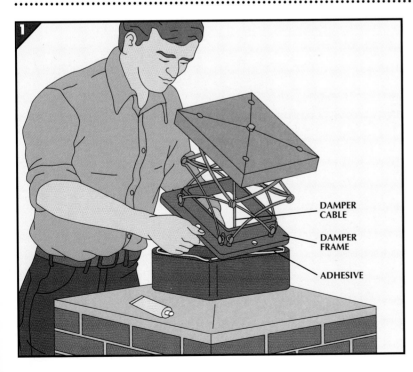

DAMPER CABLE

DAMPER FRAME

ADHESIVE

1. Securing the damper.

◆ Clean the top edges of the flue with a wire brush, then apply along the edges a $\frac{1}{4}$-inch bead of the adhesive supplied with the damper.

◆ From the top of the chimney, drop the damper cable down the flue *(left)*. Have a helper inside the house check to make sure that the cable extends all the way down into the fireplace.

◆ Press the damper frame firmly against the flue to seat it in the adhesive.

2. Mounting the cable bracket.

◆ With a $\frac{1}{4}$-inch masonry bit, drill a hole $1\frac{1}{4}$ inches deep into the firebrick near the front of the fireplace and about 20 inches off the floor.

◆ With a ball-peen hammer, secure the damper cable bracket to the brick with one of the nail anchors supplied.

◆ With the bracket in place, drill the second hole, and drive the other anchor *(above)*.

◆ Slip the chain through the hole in the bracket and thread the cable through the fitting on the end of the chain *(inset)*.

◆ Pull on the cable to close the damper, then tighten the setscrew to fix the cable.

◆ Trim off excess cable with wire cutters.

SETSCREW   CABLE

NAIL ANCHOR

CHAIN

EXTENDING THE FLUE

1. Removing the old crown.

With a ball-peen hammer and a cold chisel, break away the masonry crown around the flue liner *(right)*, angling the tip of the chisel away from the liner to avoid damaging the liner. Do not let chips fall down the flue.

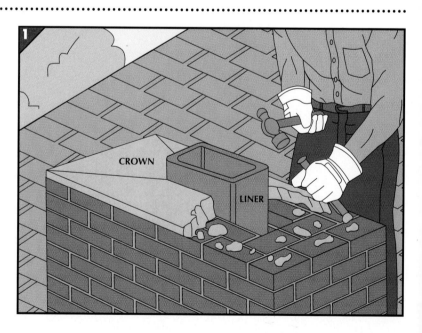

CROWN

LINER

2. Installing a flue extension.

◆ Clean the top edge of the flue liner with a wire brush, then apply fireplace mortar with a caulking gun along the edge.

◆ Position a terra-cotta liner extension squarely on top of the existing liner *(left)*.

◆ Build up the walls of the chimney with bricks *(pages 94-97)* to the height of the new liner. Add more liner sections and bricks, if necessary, ending the chimney walls 8 inches below the top of the liner.

3. Forming the crown.

◆ With 3-inch common nails, build a form of 2-by-6s around the top of the chimney so that the form hugs the sides of the chimney tightly and the boards' top edges extend about $3\frac{1}{2}$ inches above the uppermost bricks.

◆ Prepare a batch of stiff mortar *(page 60)*.

◆ Moisten the bricks, then pour the mortar into the form *(right)*, overfilling it near the flue.

4. Shaping the crown.

◆ As the mortar begins to stiffen, use a mason's trowel to slope the crown up toward the flue liner on all four sides, leaving at least 4 inches of the liner exposed *(left)*.

◆ Mist the mortar with a garden hose, then tape plastic sheeting over the crown to keep it damp over the next four days.

◆ Remove the frame when the mortar has cured.

A Stainless-Steel Chimney Lining

Adding a liner to an unlined chimney can stop smoke leaks from the mortar joints and improve the draft. You may choose to have a chimney professional install a cast-in-place liner system, but a less costly solution—and one you can undertake yourself—is putting in a stainless-steel liner. If you choose this option, first verify that your house insurance policy and local building code permit installation by a nonprofessional.

A Tailor-Made Liner: Liners usually come in 3-foot lengths that must be assembled on site. Begin by measuring from the top of the flue to the point where the flue meets the smoke chamber. Next, measure the length, width, and depth of the firebox, and the width of the chimney in both directions. Take your measurements to a fireplace supplier for a liner of the correct shape and size.

Anchoring the Liner: You will need to cut an access hole through the chimney to mount the bottom plate that secures the liner in place. For the plate, buy a sheet of 24-gauge stainless steel at least 4 inches wider and longer than the flue opening from a sheet-metal fabricator.

 TOOLS

Tape measure
Electric drill
Masonry bit
Cold chisel
Ball-peen
 hammer
Compass
Tin snips
Screwdriver
Caulking gun
Mason's trowel

 **MATERIALS**

Stainless-steel chimney
 liner (24 gauge) and
 sheet-metal screws
Stainless steel sheet
 (24 gauge)
Masonry screws (2")
Fireplace mortar cartridge
Mortar ingredients
 (Portland cement, hydrat-
 ed lime, masonry sand)
Chimney-lining insulation
Flashing metal
Chimney-rated caulk

 SAFETY TIPS

Wear safety goggles when drilling into masonry or chipping out mortar, and gloves when handling or cutting sheet metal.

ACCESS HOLE OUTLINE

1. Making an access hole in the chimney.

◆ At the top of the chimney flue, feed a 50-foot tape measure down to measure the distance from the top of the flue to the top of the smoke chamber. Have a helper shine a flashlight up the flue from inside the house to see when the tape reaches the smoke chamber. Transfer your measurement outside to mark the top of the smoke chamber on the chimney.

◆ Outline the access hole on the chimney from the mortar joint closest to the top of the smoke chamber to a height of two brick courses. Make the outline as wide as the inside width of the chimney—usually three brick lengths.

◆ Loosen the bricks within the outline by drilling through the mortar surrounding them with a masonry bit *(left)*. Pull out the bricks and set them aside.

◆ With a ball-peen hammer and cold chisel, chip off any mortar adhering to the bricks framing the access hole. Brush away debris.

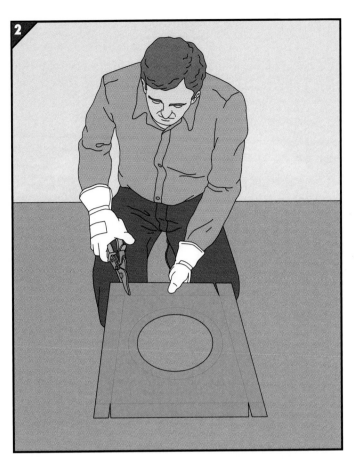

2. Sizing the bottom plate.

◆ Measure the inside dimensions of the flue at the top of the chimney and draw a matching rectangle on a sheet of 24-gauge stainless steel.

◆ Draw a second rectangle, 2 inches longer and wider, around the first.

◆ At the center of the rectangles, draw a circle of the same diameter as the chimney liner; then center a second circle, 2 inches smaller, inside the first.

◆ Cut around the outside rectangle and the inner circle with tin snips.

◆ At each corner, cut a slit from the edge to the inner rectangle, forming four parallel tabs *(left)*.

3. Shaping the plate.

◆ Make cuts at 1-inch intervals around the inside of the plate from the edge of the inner circle to the rim of the larger circle *(right)*, forming a series of tabs.

◆ Bend up the tabs at a 90-degree angle. Bend up the edges of the rectangle as well, wrapping the four tabs around the corners to form a flange around the plate *(inset)*.

◆ Working outside, slide the plate, flanges and tabs pointing upward, into the access hole in the chimney. The flanges should sit snugly against the walls of the chimney—bend the edges again, if necessary. Then position the plate in the chimney so the top edges of the flanges are flush with the tops of the bricks at the bottom of the access hole.

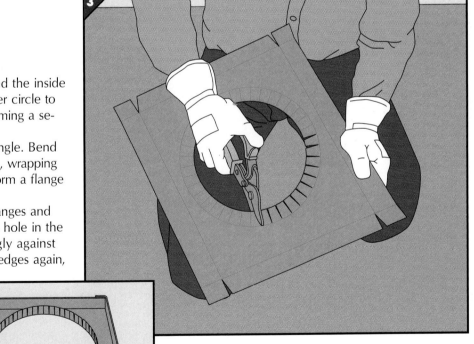

FLANGE

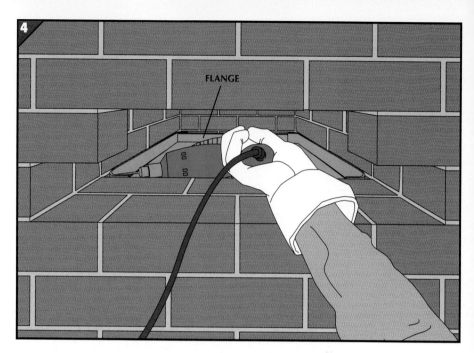

4. Anchoring the plate.

◆ Drill two $\frac{1}{4}$-inch holes through each flange *(right)*—one at the front and one at the back of the chimney—drilling into the bricks behind the flanges.

◆ Fasten the flanges to the bricks with 2-inch masonry screws. Caulk any gaps between the plate and the chimney walls with fireplace mortar.

5. Installing the chimney liner.

◆ Working on the roof with a helper, assemble the liner sections together; at each connection, use four of the screws supplied. Flexible flue liners are available for curving flues *(photograph)*. Lower the liner down the chimney until it contacts the bottom plate.

◆ Have a helper at the access hole apply fireplace mortar with a caulking gun around the inside of the bottom end of the liner and slip the liner over the tabs on the plate *(above)*.

◆ Replace the bricks in the access hole, mortaring them in place *(pages 57-58)*.

◆ To insulate the liner, buy chimney-lining insulation and pour it down the chimney, filling the space around the liner from the bottom plate to the top of the chimney.

◆ Seal the gap between the liner and the flue at the top of the chimney with a cap made from a piece of flashing metal cut 1 inch longer and wider than the flue opening. Cut a hole through the cap for the liner and run a bead of chimney-rated caulk around the top edge of the flue. Slip the cap over the liner and press it down onto the flue. Caulk the joint between the cap and the liner.

Returning an old wood-burning stove to good working order can be gratifying, but keep in mind that its performance will pale in comparison to that of a modern advanced-combustion or catalytic stove. If you plan to use a stove as a primary heat source, a modern stove or heater is a wiser choice *(pages 32-35)*.

Inspecting the Exterior: Before buying a secondhand stove, examine it thoroughly. Check the bottom to make sure that the legs provide stable support and the stove sits firmly on its base. Missing bolts or cracks in the legs are not fatal flaws—bolts can be replaced and a cracked leg can be welded at a foundry. Although cracks in the body of a stove can be repaired *(below)*, avoid purchasing a stove with anything larger than a hairline crack.

An Internal Exam: Inside the stove, check the floor lining— either firebricks or metal—for wear. On a stove with a circular floor, a castable lining will work best; buy the mix from a chimney-supply store and pour it onto the stove's floor. Otherwise, replace or add firebricks *(page 27)*.

Check the stove's movable parts —baffle, door handles, and draft controls. If parts are sluggish, a thorough cleaning may restore them to order. Missing door glass or gaskets are easy to replace *(page 27)*, but if anything else is missing from the stove, think twice about buying it; replacement parts are nearly impossible to find and costly to have made.

If the stove comes with a house you are buying, inspect the installation. It should meet the same standards that apply to a new set-up *(pages 36-42)*.

TOOLS

Work light	Ball-peen hammer
Wire brush	Screwdriver
Putty knife	Tape measure
Shoe brush	Heavy-duty
Brick set	scissors
	Utility knife

MATERIALS

	Firebricks
Furnace cement	Ceramic stove
Stove blacking	window
Metal polish	Stove door gaskets
	Gasket cement

SAFETY TIPS

Wear gloves when removing a broken stove window; add goggles when cutting firebricks.

SEALING CRACKS IN A FIREBOX

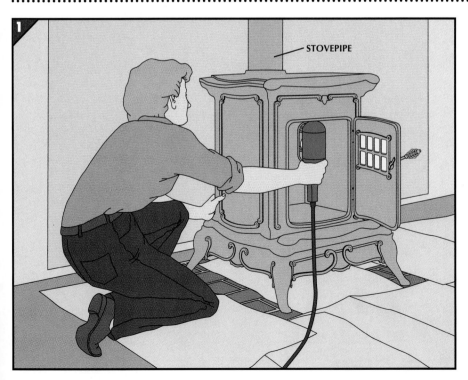

STOVEPIPE

1. Locating the cracks.
◆ Place newspaper on the floor around the stove. Remove any grates, baffles, or movable linings from the stove's interior, then hang a work light in the firebox *(left)*.
◆ Close the stove's door, turn off the room lights, and check the seams between sections of the stove body for leaking light.
◆ Disconnect the stovepipe *(page 114)*, then have a helper tilt the stove so you can inspect the underside for leaks. To check for cracks that are too fine to pass light, rub chalk lightly over the stove's surface; the chalk will fill any crack, leaving a visible line. Or, you can light a small fire in the stove and watch for wisps of smoke seeping out.

FURNACE
CEMENT

2. Caulking a crack.

◆ With a wire brush, remove any rust or loose dirt from around the crack both inside and outside the stove.

◆ On the outside, outline the crack with masking tape to protect the surrounding surface from the furnace cement.

◆ Inside, dampen the damaged area with a wet cloth or sponge, then pack furnace cement into the crack with a putty knife. Repeat the process on the outside *(above)*.

◆ Remove the tape and let the cement dry for 24 hours. When using the stove next, keep a small kindling fire going for 2 hours to check the repair.

CORRECTING MINOR FLAWS

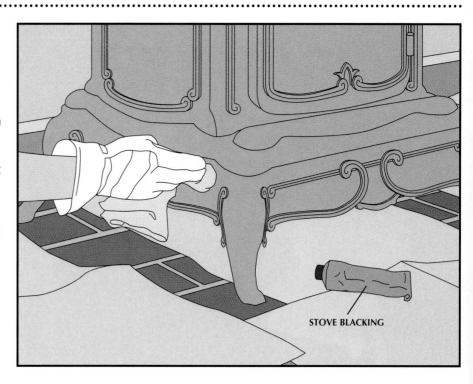

STOVE BLACKING

Polishing a worn stove.

◆ Remove encrusted dirt and rust from the stove's exterior by scrubbing the surface with a wire brush.

◆ For cast-iron sections, rub a light coat of stove blacking over the surface with a soft cloth *(right)*. Once the blacking dries, buff the metal with a shoe brush.

◆ Restore the shine to any nickel-plated parts with ordinary metal polish.

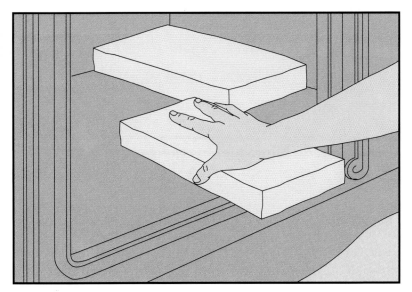

Lining a stove.

◆ Starting at the back and working toward the door, lay a dry run of firebricks on the firebox floor. Place the bricks in rows, spacing the units $\frac{1}{8}$ inch apart *(left)*. Cut bricks *(page 59)* as necessary to cover the floor, but don't try to fill small, irregular spaces at the edge of the firebox.

◆ Remove the bricks, noting their position in the stove. With a putty knife, apply furnace cement to the edges that will contact other bricks—don't apply cement to brick surfaces that will abut the floor or walls of the stove. Reposition the bricks in the stove.

◆ Let the cement dry for at least 24 hours before lighting a fire in the stove.

Replacing a stove window.

◆ Remove the screws securing the back plate over the window, and slip out the old pane.

◆ Order a clear-ceramic pane to fit the door—it should be about $\frac{1}{4}$ inch wider and longer than the opening.

◆ Center the pane over the opening, reposition the back plate over the glass *(right)*, then fasten the back plate in place.

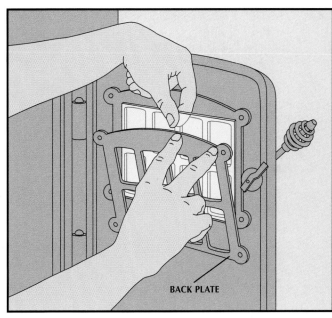

BACK PLATE

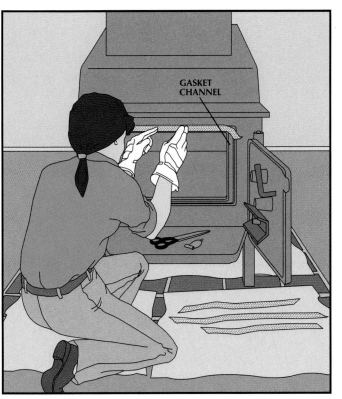

GASKET CHANNEL

Replacing a gasket.

◆ Pull off the old gasket around the stove's door opening. Clean out the gasket channel with a wire brush or a putty knife.

◆ Buy a length of tubular or flat fiberglass gasket that matches the original. Measure and cut four strips of the gasket to span the edges of the opening, making each piece about 1 inch longer than the actual measurement.

◆ Beginning at the top of the opening, squeeze a bead of gasket cement into the channel and press the gasket into place *(left)*.

◆ Repeat on the other sides, mitering the ends of the strips with a utility knife so they meet squarely at the corners.

◆ Let the cement dry for 24 hours before using the stove.

Fans and Registers to Circulate Heat

The warm air from a wood stove or fireplace will spread more easily throughout a house equipped with a system of fans and registers *(page 9)*.

Ceiling Fans: A common style of fan is illustrated below, but there are many variations; follow the manufacturer's instructions for the model you buy. Most fans can be located in place of an existing light fixture, although the electrical box will have to be replaced with one rated for ceiling fans. To bear the extra weight, the box must be either secured to a joist or anchored to a bar hanger, which fastens to the joists on either side of the box.

Registers: These units permit air to flow from one room to another, either by natural draft or by the work of fans. The registers have wide louvers or open grilles that let air pass through easily *(opposite)*.

⚠ **CAUTION** *Never work on a live circuit: Switch off power to it at the service panel, then check all wires with a voltage tester.*

⚠ **CAUTION** *When cutting into walls, floors, or ceilings, take precautions against releasing lead and asbestos particles into the air* (page 36).

TOOLS

Screwdriver
Saber saw

MATERIALS

Electrical box rated
    for fan support
Wire caps
Electrical wire
Two-part wall
    register kit

REPLACING A LIGHT FIXTURE WITH A CEILING FAN

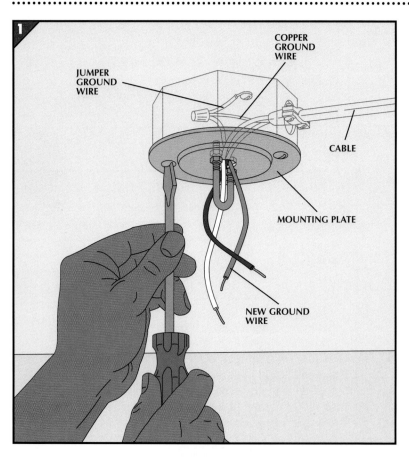

1

JUMPER
GROUND
WIRE

COPPER
GROUND
WIRE

CABLE

MOUNTING PLATE

NEW GROUND
WIRE

1. Securing the mounting plate.

◆ Turn off power to the electrical box at the service panel.

◆ Remove the old fixture and disconnect its wires from those in the existing electrical box. Remove the box and replace it with one specifically designed to support a fan; fasten it securely to a joist. Alternatively, install a box on a bar hanger made for a ceiling fan.

◆ Unscrew the jumper ground wire from the old box and attach it to the new box. Then, with a wire cap, join it to the bare copper ground wire from the cable along with a new piece of ground wire.

◆ Thread the cable wires and the new ground wire through the fan mounting plate.

◆ Fasten the mounting plate to the box *(left)*.

2. Hanging the fan.

◆ Hook the fan's rubber wheel on the mounting plate's U-shaped bracket. Insert the shaft through the rubber wheel and secure it with a cotter pin.

◆ Using wire caps of the appropriate size, make the connections—black wire to black, white to white, and the ground wire to the fan's ground wire *(right)*.

◆ Turn on the power to test the fan, then turn it off immediately.

◆ Cover the wires by raising the canopy to within $\frac{1}{8}$ inch of the ceiling and fastening it in place.

◆ Attach the fan blades to the blade holders then restore the power.

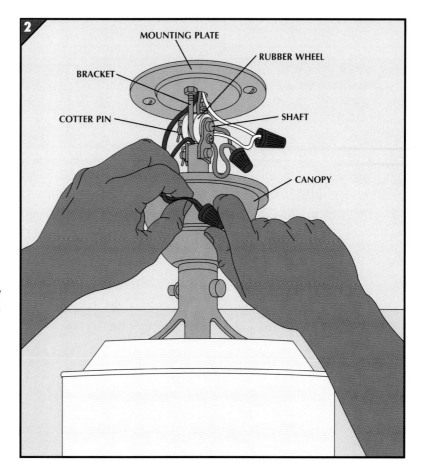

MOUNTING PLATE
RUBBER WHEEL
BRACKET
COTTER PIN
SHAFT
CANOPY

INSTALLING A WALL REGISTER

Attaching the grilles.

◆ With a saber saw, cut matching openings, sized for the register, on both sides of the wall between two studs.

◆ From each side of the wall, slide one piece of a two-part register into place *(left)*. Fasten the pieces to the wall with the screws supplied.

A floor register *(photograph)* can be installed in a similar manner between two joists.

Wood Stoves and Factory-Built Fireplaces

2

One of the best ways to heat a home with wood is with a wood-burning stove. This chapter will help you select a stove to suit your needs, and describes how to install a typical model. A fireplace insert and a factory-built fireplace are two alternatives that combine the look of a fireplace with the efficiency of a stove.

Cutting an opening for a flue liner →

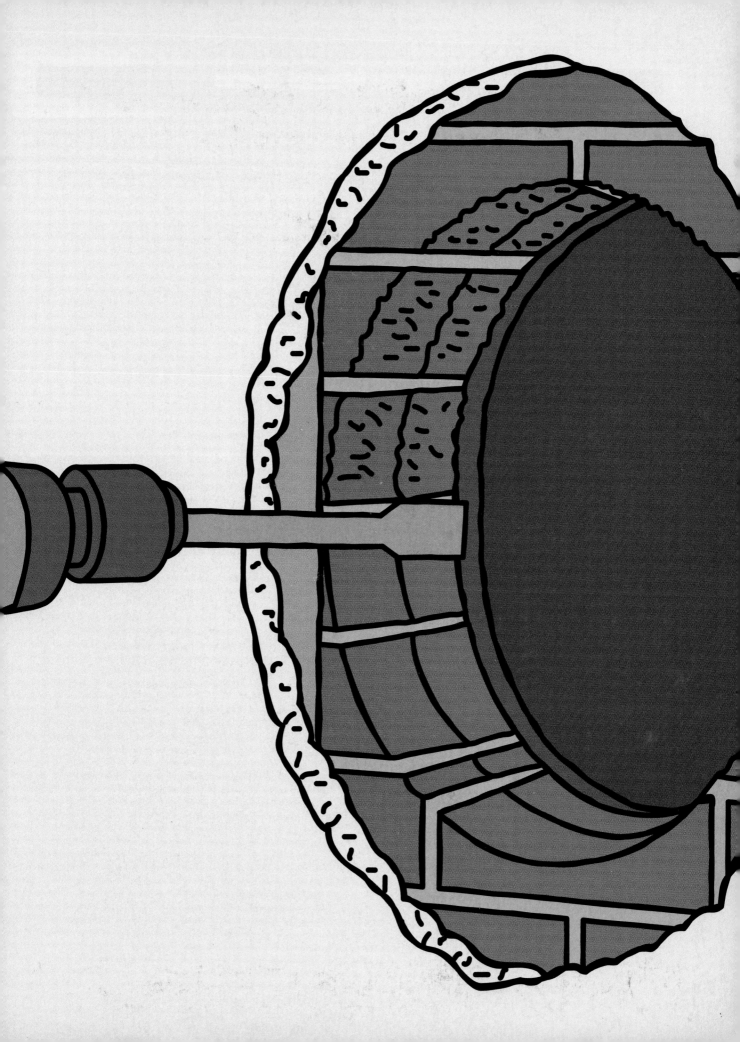

Choosing an Efficient Heater

The two most important concerns in evaluating a stove that will serve as a primary heat source are its heating efficiency and heating capacity. One is a function of the stove's physical components, the other of its design; but the two are closely related.

Heating Efficiency: The heating efficiency of a stove is a measure of the stove's ability to extract heat from a given amount of wood. It is usually expressed as the percentage of potential energy released by the burning wood within the stove, as opposed to the energy that goes up the flue in the form of hot air and combustible but unburned gases. Modern stoves ranges from 50 percent to more than 70 percent.

Heating Capacity: The heating capacity of a stove is measured by its output of British Thermal Units (BTUs) per hour. A stove rated at 20,000 BTUs, for example, should comfortably heat a 15-by-18-foot room. But doors, windows, ceiling height, insulation, and outdoor temperatures can influence the figure.

Buying a Stove: Resist the temptation to buy a stove that is too large for the area to be heated—your home will be uncomfortably hot. To find a stove ideal for your home, consult stove suppliers as well as neighbors who have wood stoves.

TWO STOVES THAT CONSERVE FUEL

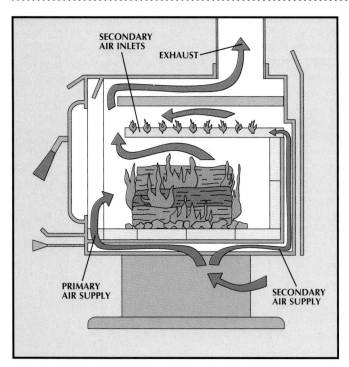

Advanced combustion.
Smoke contains volatile gases that ignite at a higher temperature than does wood *(page 8)*. An advanced combustion stove is designed to burn these gases before they enter the flue. A secondary source of air provides oxygen for the ignition of the gases at the secondary air inlets.

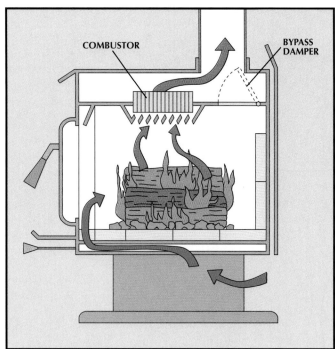

Catalytic burning.
This type of stove features a combustor, which causes the volatile gases to ignite as they pass through it. A bypass damper can be opened when starting a fire to increase airflow. The combustor must be replaced periodically; the coating can be destroyed if certain plastics are burned in the stove.

DESIGNS THAT STRESS HEAT OUTPUT

Radiant stoves.
A radiant stove usually has thick cast-iron or steel sides that transmit heat in all directions. These stoves work best centrally located in an open-home plan where the heat will disperse throughout the house *(page 9)*. In a more confined area, they can make a room uncomfortably hot.

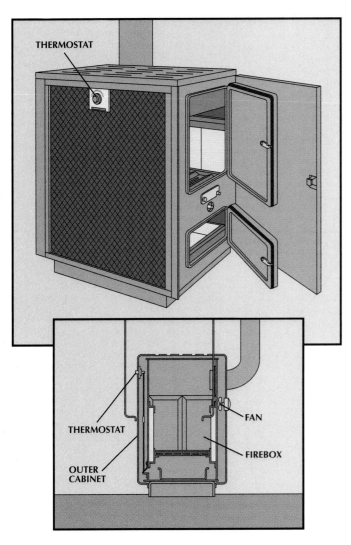

THERMOSTAT

Convection stoves.
A convection, or circulating, stove has a cast-iron or steel firebox encased in a sheet-metal cabinet. Ambient air, moved by convection patterns or a fan, passes between the firebox and the cabinet *(inset)* to be heated and returned to the room. The thermostat linked to the primary air intake automatically regulates the fire's air supply.

THERMOSTAT

FAN

FIREBOX

OUTER CABINET

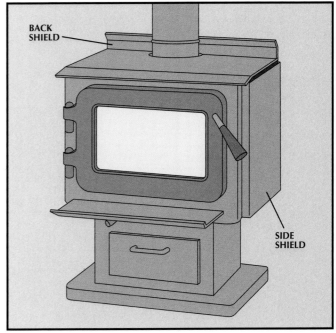

BACK SHIELD

SIDE SHIELD

Combination stoves.
These stoves combine elements of both radiant and convection stoves. The top and front radiate heat directly. Meanwhile, room air passes behind shields on the back and sides, creating warm currents.

THE COOKSTOVE

A dual-purpose stove.

While not quite as practical as stoves designed solely for heating, modern cookstoves heat very well. With an airtight firebox and gasket-sealed doors, they are much more efficient than their antique predecessors. And according to experienced cookstove chefs, the even heat that radiates from their cast-iron walls bakes better than any other kind of stove. The warming ovens situated over the burners keep food hot naturally.

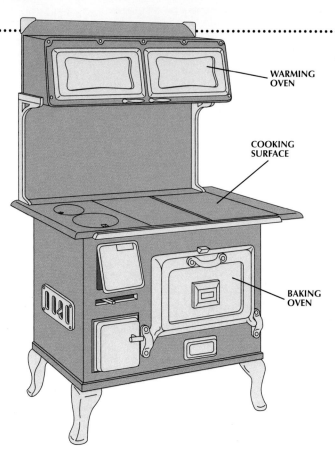

WARMING OVEN

COOKING SURFACE

BAKING OVEN

THE PELLET STOVE

A convenient fuel source.

Clean-burning and extremely efficient, these stoves consume pellets made of compressed sawdust. An auger transfers pellets from a hopper into the fire chamber at a controlled rate (inset); fans expel warm air through a heat-exchange pipe and exhaust air through an outlet in the back of the stove. The hopper can hold up to 65 pounds of pellets—enough to burn steadily for 48 hours. The main drawback to this type of stove is that it relies on electricity to operate the auger and fans; unless equipped with a backup battery, a pellet stove will not function during a power outage.

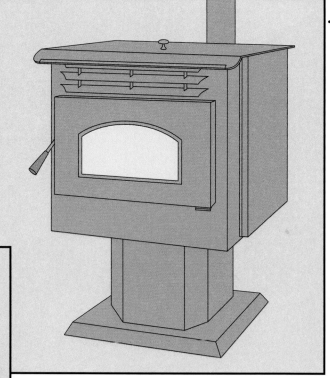

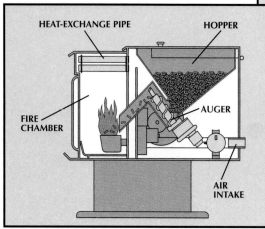

HEAT-EXCHANGE PIPE

HOPPER

FIRE CHAMBER

AUGER

AIR INTAKE

Fireplace inserts.

Essentially a wood stove designed to fit into an existing fireplace opening, the insert retains the look and feel of a traditional fireplace while greatly improving the heating performance. Modern fireplace inserts burn cleanly and, with sophisticated heat exchangers, are nearly as efficient as freestanding stoves.

Order a style that fits into your fireplace, allowing for all clearances suggested by the manufacturer (page 43-45). Install a flue liner that matches the draft requirements of the stove.

Factory-made fireplaces.

Like fireplace inserts, factory-made or prefab fireplaces can be as efficient as wood stoves. They employ either a catalytic converter or advanced combustion burning technique. Air is drawn in at the bottom, heated by the fireplace, and returned into the room from the top.

Installing one of these heaters requires only basic carpentry skills—no knowledge of masonry techniques is needed. A brick facade can be added to create a traditional look.

Masonry heaters.

Despite its outward appearance, a masonry heater functions differently from a fireplace. The firebox is sheathed by concrete and bricks. A very intense but short-lived fire is burned in the firebox, and the mass of masonry absorbs the heat and slowly radiates it back into the house. Smoke and exhaust drift through a maze of channels in the heater before leaving via the flue. Generally, only two fires per day are needed to keep a house warm. Masonry heaters are usually installed by a professional.

Installing a Wood Stove

Adding the warmth and character of a wood stove to an average home takes about a weekend's work. The most difficult job is cutting passageways for the stovepipe.

Positioning the Stove: Select the area of the house that will offer the most heating efficiency (pages 8-9). Pick a spot where the flue can rise straight to the roof without bending; this will help the chimney develop a good draft and stay clean. You will also need to observe local building code requirements as well as the recommendations of the stove manufacturer regarding clearance between the stove and the house walls or other combustible materials. In general, allow at least 36 inches from the sides and rear of the stove and 60 inches above it.

Heat Protection: Clearance requirements can be relaxed with the use of heat shields made of sheet metal, copper, or other materials (opposite). Again, check your code. The accessories required to mount the shields (page 38) are available at a fireplace supplier.

The wood stove will need a hearth to protect the floor from stray embers. Options include bricks laid dry over sheet metal (page 39), mortared bricks, grouted ceramic tiles, or prefabricated insulating hearths.

A Metal Chimney: For the stove's venting system, you will need stovepipe long enough to reach from the base of the stove's flue collar to within 1 inch of the ceiling. Codes typically require insulated chimney pipe to be installed above the ceiling in place of the stovepipe. Components for the safe passage of the chimney through house walls, floors, and roofs are illustrated opposite.

 TOOLS

Plumb bob
Tape measure
Ruler
Electronic
  stud finder
Electric drill
Screwdriver bit
Hammer
Utility knife

Brick set
Ball-peen hammer
Compass saw
Utility knife
Straightedge
Saber saw
Clamps
Carpenter's level
Hacksaw
Putty knife
Prybar

 MATERIALS

Heat shield
Ceramic spacers
  and screws
Contact cement
Sheet metal
  (24 gauge)
Bricks
1 x 2s, 2 x 4s
Joist lumber
Common nails
  (2", $3\frac{1}{2}$")

Roofing nails ($1\frac{1}{2}$")
Sheet-metal screws
  ($\frac{1}{2}$" No. 8)
Stovepipe sections
Insulated chimney
  pipe
Chimney-pipe
  support
Chimney-flue
  flashing
Roofing cement
Storm collar
Chimney cap

 SAFETY TIPS

Wear goggles when operating a drill or driving nails.

 CAUTION

Lead and asbestos, known health hazards, pervade houses built or remodeled before 1978. Lead is found primarily in paint; asbestos may be present in wallboard, joint compound, insulation, flooring and related adhesives, roofing materials, and flashing. Before cutting into walls, floors, or roofs, mist the area with a solution of 1 teaspoon of low-sudsing detergent per quart of water, then cut out a small piece with a hand tool. Use a home test kit for lead; take asbestos samples to a certified lab. If either substance is present, you may want to hire a professional for the job; if you do the work yourself, follow these procedures:

! *Keep people and pets out of the work area.*

! *Wear protective clothing (available from a safety equipment store) and a dual-cartridge respirator with high-efficiency particulate air (HEPA) filters. Remove the clothing before leaving the work area, wash it separately, and shower immediately.*

! *Indoors, seal off work area openings including windows, doors, vents, and air conditioners with 6-mil polyethylene sheeting and duct tape. Cover rugs and nonmovable items with sheeting and tape, and turn off forced-air systems. Mop twice when the job is done. Outdoors, don't work in windy conditions, and cover the ground around the area with plastic sheeting.*

! *Never sand materials or cut them with power tools; mist them with detergent and remove them with a hand tool.*

! *Place all debris a 6-mil polyethylene bag and call your health department or environmental protection agency for disposal regulations.*

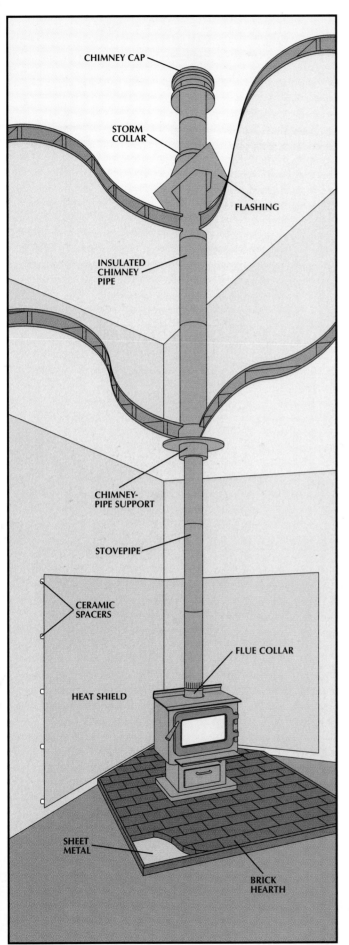

CHIMNEY CAP

STORM COLLAR

FLASHING

INSULATED CHIMNEY PIPE

CHIMNEY-PIPE SUPPORT

STOVEPIPE

CERAMIC SPACERS

FLUE COLLAR

HEAT SHIELD

SHEET METAL

BRICK HEARTH

A stove system.

The heart of this heating system is a high-efficiency wood stove resting on a brick hearth set on a layer of sheet metal. A heat shield behind the stove, held just above the surface of the wall with ceramic spacers, protects the surrounding walls. The vent system begins at the stove's flue collar and runs straight up through the roof. The uninsulated stovepipe meets the insulated chimney pipe inside a chimney-pipe support at the ceiling. At the roof, flashing braces the chimney pipe and, with the storm collar above it, keeps the opening weathertight. A chimney cap keeps out rain and debris and limits downdrafts.

REDUCING CLEARANCES WITH SHIELDS

Type of Shield	Amount of Reduction	
	Sides and Rear	**Top**
Sheet metal (24 gauge or thicker)	67%	50%
Ceramic tiles	50%	33%
Ceramic tiles with sheet-metal backing	67%	50%
Bricks	50%	N/A
Bricks with sheet-metal backing	67%	N/A
Prefab heat shields	67%	67%

Selecting heat shields.

Local building codes and stove manufacturers regulate clearances between stoves and nearby combustibles such as walls. If you add a heat shield, you can locate the stove closer to these combustibles than the standard clearance. The chart above shows the percentage you can reduce the distance depending on the material of the shield. Check codes for guidelines on how much air space is required between the shield and the wall and at the shield's top and bottom.

PUTTING UP HEAT SHIELDS

1. Positioning the stove.

◆ Place the stove in the desired position—being sure to allow for the required clearances *(page 37)*—and drop a plumb bob from the ceiling to the center of the flue opening *(right)*.

◆ Mark the ceiling at the top of the plumb line and use a stud finder to mark the joists on each side of the line.

◆ Midway between the two joists, establish a new center point for the flue opening. Hang the line from this point and reposition the stove to center its flue opening under the bob. If the stove is now too close to a wall or other combustible, center the opening under the next pair of joists.

◆ With a ruler, outline a ceiling opening around the center point that matches the framing measurements for the chimney-pipe support—$1\frac{1}{2}$ inches more on all sides than the pipe-support diameter.

◆ Outline the base of the stove on the floor, then move the stove out of the way.

FLUE OPENING

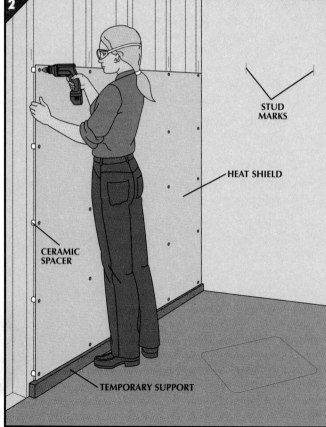

STUD MARKS

HEAT SHIELD

CERAMIC SPACER

TEMPORARY SUPPORT

2. Mounting the shields.

◆ Have 24-gauge sheet metal cut to the dimensions specified by your local building code. The shield typically must extend 18 inches on each side of the stove and 20 inches above its top. In addition, no edge of the shield should extend more than 2 inches beyond a wall stud.

◆ With a stud finder, mark the wall studs that the shield will cover.

◆ Position a shield against the wall and transfer the stud locations to the back. Draw a line down the back of the shield at each stud mark.

◆ Drill a hole through the shield 1 inch from the top and bottom of each line and every 16 inches in between.

◆ With contact cement, fasten a ceramic spacer to the back of the shield at each hole.

◆ Place a board on the floor to support the shield 1 inch above the planned height of the hearth, hold the shield against the wall so the spacers align with the studs, and fasten the shield through the holes with the screws supplied with the spacers *(left)*.

BUILDING THE HEARTH

HEARTH BASE

Placing the bricks.

◆ Around the stove outline, mark the perimeter of the hearth on the floor so it extends at least 18 inches beyond the stove front and 8 inches beyond the sides and back. Adjust the layout so its length and width are multiples of actual brick dimensions. Have a sheet of 24-gauge metal cut to match the layout.

◆ Note the stove location by measuring the distances between it and the adjoining walls, then set the metal base on the floor.

◆ Cover the base with bricks laid end to end *(above)*. Stagger the joints between rows by starting every second row with a half brick *(page 59)*. Some bricks will need to be cut at an angle to fit against the wall.

◆ Surround the bricks with a frame of 1-by-2s set on edge. Miter the ends of boards as needed to butt flush against the wall, and toenail the boards to the wall with 2-inch common nails.

EXTENDING THE FLUE THROUGH THE ROOF

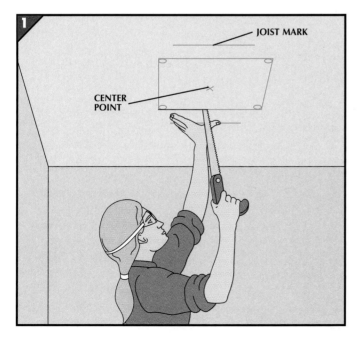

JOIST MARK

CENTER POINT

1. Opening the ceiling.

◆ Turn off the power to the work area at the service panel, and take care to avoid cutting into wiring.

◆ Cut through the ceiling along the outline marked on page 38 *(Step 1)*. For wallboard, drill a $\frac{1}{2}$-inch hole at each corner of the outline, then cut along the lines with a compass saw *(left)*. For plaster, cover the outline with masking tape and score it with a utility knife and a straightedge. Drill $\frac{1}{2}$-inch starting holes at the corners and cut along the scored lines with a compass saw.

◆ Once the section of ceiling has been removed, drill $\frac{1}{2}$-inch pilot holes through the floor above at all four corners of the opening.

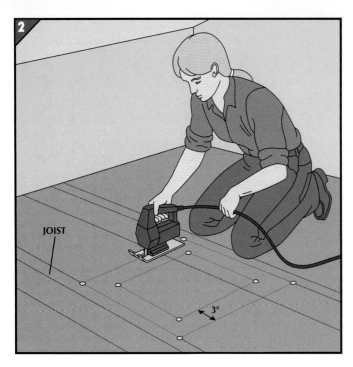

2. Cutting through the floor.

◆ Outline an opening on the floor above, using the holes drilled in Step 1 as corners.

◆ Enlarge the outline on the sides perpendicular to the joists by 3 inches.

◆ Enlarge the outline on the remaining sides so they are flush with the joists, which you can locate with a stud finder. Drill new corner holes, then cut around the new outline with a saber saw *(left)*.

JOIST

3"

3. Framing the opening.

◆ From lumber the same dimensions as the joists, cut two braces to fit in between the joists.

◆ Fit each brace between the joists with its outside face flush with the opening in the ceiling below, then toenail it to the joists with $3\frac{1}{2}$-inch common nails *(right)*.

◆ Nail support blocks to the joists between the braces to build the joists out flush with the sides of the ceiling opening below.

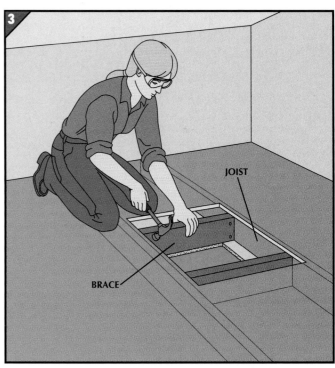

JOIST

BRACE

CHIMNEY-SUPPORT CYLINDER

SUPPORT BLOCK

4. Fitting the chimney-pipe support.

◆ Have a helper push the chimney-pipe support up through the framed opening so its collar butts against the ceiling. Clamp the support to each brace.

◆ Cut a 2-by-4 slightly longer than the cylinder diameter and set the board across the support.

◆ Place a level on the board and reposition the cylinder, if necessary, to level it *(left)*. Rotate the level 90 degrees and check it again.

◆ Fasten the cylinder to the support blocks through the predrilled holes with 2-inch nails.

◆ Remove the clamps and nail the cylinder to the braces.

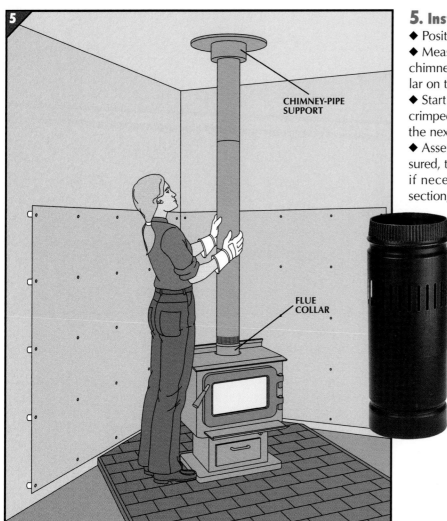

5. Installing the stovepipe.
◆ Position the stove on the hearth.
◆ Measure the distance from the bottom of the chimney-pipe support to the base of the flue collar on the stove and add $2\frac{1}{2}$ inches.
◆ Start with the bottom section of stovepipe, crimped end down, and slide the crimped end of the next section into the top of the first.
◆ Assemble the sections to the distance you measured, trimming the top section with a hacksaw if necessary; or consider installing a telescoping section, which opens up for easy cleaning access *(photograph)*.
◆ Drill three pilot holes through the pieces, then secure them together with $\frac{1}{2}$-inch No. 8 sheet-metal screws.
◆ Slip the top end of the stovepipe up into the chimney-pipe support, and push the bottom end firmly down into the flue collar *(left)*.
◆ Drill four pilot holes through the flanged end of the support into the stovepipe, then fasten the joint together with screws.

6. Cutting through the roof.
◆ Inside the attic, hang a plumb bob over one corner of the floor opening and mark the ceiling at this point. Repeat at the remaining three corners.
◆ At each point, drive a nail through the ceiling and roofing.
◆ Working safely on the roof *(page 18)*, outline the rectangle formed by the nails.
◆ Cut away the shingles and roofing felt within the outline using a utility knife *(right)*, then remove the roof sheathing with a saber saw or a compass saw.

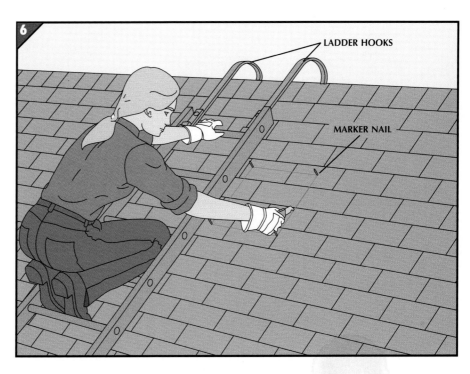

FLASHING OUTLINE

CHIMNEY-FLUE FLASHING

7. Installing the chimney-flue flashing.

◆ Center the flashing over the opening and trace its outline on the roof. Draw a second outline 3 inches inside the first *(above, left)*. Cut through the shingles along the top two-thirds of the smaller rectangle with a utility knife and clear away the shingles.

◆ With a putty knife, spread roofing cement on the shingles around the lower third of the smaller rectangle.

◆ Slide the flashing up under the shingles along the top two-thirds of the outline *(above, right)*, prying out any roofing nails that are in the way. Press the lower edge of the flashing onto the cement-coated shingles.

◆ Lift the loose edges of the shingles around the top of the flashing and fasten the flashing to the roof sheathing at 3-inch intervals with $1\frac{1}{2}$-inch roofing nails. Nail the lower part of the flashing sides, but not the bottom end, to the shingles. Cover the nailheads with roofing cement.

CHIMNEY PIPE

STORM COLLAR

8. Adding the storm collar and cap.

◆ Working inside, assemble sections of insulated chimney pipe from the chimney-pipe support up through the roof and flashing.

◆ Slip the storm collar over the pipe so it comes into contact with the flashing *(above)*. Cover the joint between the collar and the pipe above it with roofing cement.

◆ Lengthen the chimney pipe as necessary with additional sections so it extends at least 3 feet above the roof adjoining it on the uproof side, and 2 feet above any other obstacle within 10 feet, such as the roof ridge. With a roof brace—available from chimney suppliers—anchor the pipe to the roof if it extends more than 4 feet above the roof.

◆ Install a chimney cap on the top of the pipe.

Inside the house, you may be required by code to build a small stud-wall enclosure called a chase around the section of chimney pipe that runs through any second-story or attic room *(inset)*.

An unused fireplace can be salvaged to provide supplementary heat. The fireplace itself presents a ready-made cavity for a fireplace insert *(below and pages 44-45)*, or you can tap the old chimney to serve as a flue for a freestanding stove *(pages 46-47)*. For either of these projects, observe all code and safety requirements that apply to fireplaces or freestanding stoves.

Clearances: Before buying a fireplace insert, measure the height, width, and depth of the firebox. Inserts need minimum clearances, specified by the manufacturer, between the appliance and the firebox walls. Clearances to combustibles—such as a wooden mantel—must also meet the minimum. Since inserts produce more heat than an open fireplace, have the firebox and chimney inspected before beginning, to ensure they are in perfect repair.

Flue Liners: Fireplace inserts require a direct connection to the flue with a flexible liner running from the appliance collar through the damper and smoke chamber. The best method is to remove the damper and run the liner all the way up the chimney. Not only will the liner create better draft, the system can also be cleaned with less effort.

Freestanding Stoves: To vent a stove into an existing chimney, you must cut a hole in the chimney and anchor a stovepipe adapter called a thimble in the opening. Again, have a professional assess the project before you begin, to determine whether your existing chimney is adequate.

⚠️ **CAUTION** *Before cutting through your walls, ceilings, or roof, take precautions against releasing lead and asbestos particles into the air (page 36).*

 TOOLS

Carpenter's level	Caulking gun
Pliers or wrench	Stud finder
Tin snips	Saber saw
Electric drill	Rotary hammer
Screwdriver	Masonry bit
	Cold chisel bit

 **MATERIALS**

Flexible flue liner	Chimney-rated caulk	Fireplace mortar
Flashing/chimney cap assembly	Thimble adapter	Lead anchors
Flue collar adapter	Slip connector	Wood screws ($1\frac{1}{2}$" No. 8)
	Collar	Sheet-metal screws ($\frac{3}{4}$" No. 8)
	Trim piece	

 SAFETY TIPS

Goggles protect your eyes when you are cutting into or chiseling masonry.

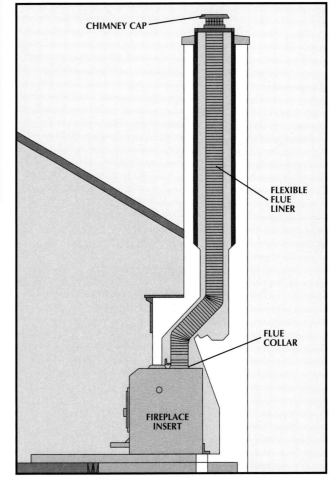

Anatomy of a fireplace insert.
The insert sits in the firebox of the existing fireplace, and the flue liner is attached to the insert's flue collar at the bottom and to a chimney cap at the top. A flexible stainless steel liner is well suited to snaking around bending flues *(right)*. The insert can be repositioned slightly after the liner has been attached to the flue collar.

CHIMNEY CAP

FLEXIBLE FLUE LINER

FLUE COLLAR

FIREPLACE INSERT

ADDING A FIREPLACE INSERT

FLUE COLLAR

CARDBOARD

1. Positioning the new firebox.
◆ Protect the hearth with a piece of heavy cardboard. Then, working with a helper, lift the insert onto the cardboard and slide it toward the rear wall of the fireplace *(left)*, observing any clearances specified by the manufacturer.
◆ Center the unit in the opening and check whether it is level; some models have adjustable legs.
◆ Buy a flexible flue liner and a flashing-and-chimney-cap assembly sized to fit your chimney flue *(page 22)*; you'll also need an adapter to attach the liner to the firebox's flue collar.
◆ Remove the damper *(page 111)* and slide the flue liner down through the top of the chimney. Have a helper fit the bottom end into the flue collar adapter on the firebox.
◆ At the top of the chimney, trim off the excess flue liner with tin snips.
◆ Drill pilot holes through the flue liner and cap assembly, then attach the pieces with the screws supplied.

2. Adding the extenders.
◆ With chalk, mark lines along the top and sides of the insert in line with the front of the fireplace opening. Then, pull out the insert just enough to access the predrilled holes on the top and sides.
◆ Loosely fasten the top extender panel to the insert with the screws supplied. Position the panel so it just covers the chalk line, then tighten the screws *(right)*. Attach the side panels the same way, lining them up with the top panel.

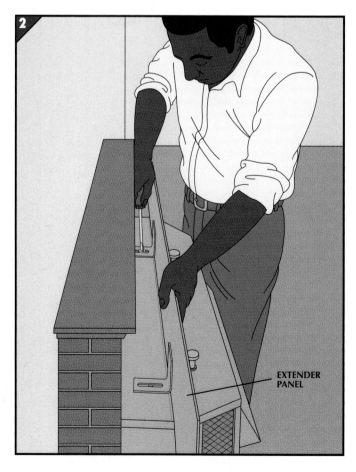

EXTENDER PANEL

3. Caulking and insulating.

◆ Apply a bead of chimney-rated caulk along the joints between the insert and the three extender panels. Also caulk the seams between the top and side panels.

◆ Attach the insulation strips supplied to the back of the panels, $\frac{1}{2}$ inch inside their outer edges *(right)*. On some models, the extender panels have special channels for these bands of insulation.

◆ Slide the insert back in the fireplace so the extender panels rest flat against the front of the opening. For an irregular hearth, it may be necessary to add insulation for a snug fit.

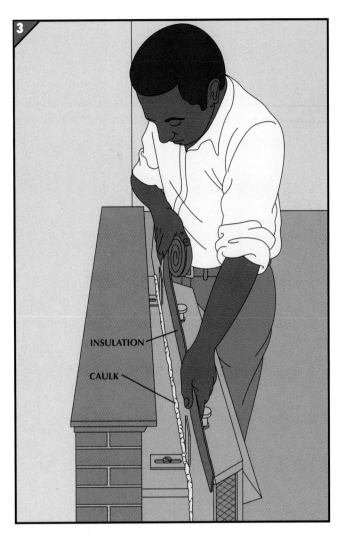

INSULATION

CAULK

GAS FIREPLACE INSERTS

Clean, reliable, and readily available, natural gas is a popular alternative fuel to wood. Fireplace inserts that burn gas *(right)* are installed much like the wood-burning insert described above, but a separate vent must be added for air intake. Some models, called "direct vent," can expel exhaust through the wall only a few feet above the fireplace, eliminating the need to pass a long liner through the chimney. Avoid any model that does not have a dedicated means to vent exhaust gases.

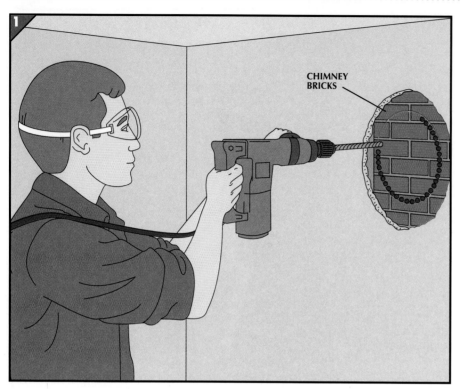

CHIMNEY BRICKS

1. Opening the flue.

◆ If the chimney is not exposed inside the house, work outside to measure from the chimney to the edge of a window and transfer the measurement inside. At the point where you want to tap into the flue and at least 18 inches below the ceiling, use a saber saw or compass saw to cut a circular section out of the finished wall a few inches larger than the diameter of the thimble *(Step 3)*.

◆ On the chimney bricks, outline a circle 1 inch larger than the thimble diameter. Then, with a long-shank $\frac{1}{2}$-inch masonry bit in a rotary hammer, drill a ring of closely spaced holes just inside the circle *(left)*, penetrating the chimney bricks and the inside wall of the flue.

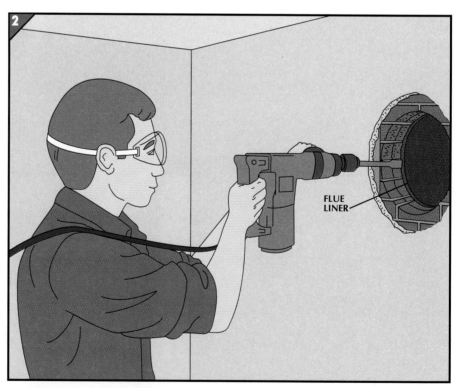

FLUE LINER

2. Shaping the opening.

◆ Install a cold chisel in the rotary hammer, select the hammer-action setting, and chip away the chimney bricks and the inside wall of the flue liner within the ring of holes *(above)*. Make the sides of the opening as smooth and regular as possible.

◆ Measure the distance from the face of the finished wall to the inside wall of the flue and order a thimble 2 inches longer.

3. Installing the thimble.

◆ Push the thimble into the hole so it projects past the wall covering by about $1\frac{1}{2}$ inches *(right)*.

◆ Reach through the thimble and, with your fingers, spread fireplace mortar between the flange at the far end of the thimble and the inside wall of the flue, sealing any gaps between the thimble and the flue.

◆ With a caulking gun, force the mortar into the space between the thimble and the chimney brick.

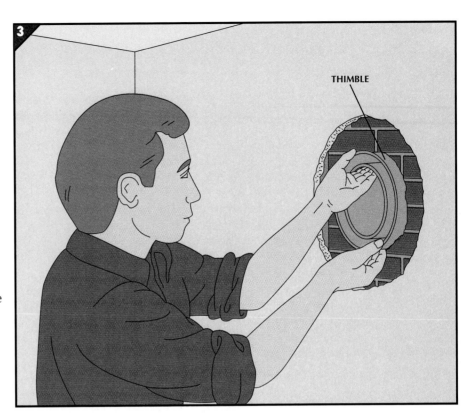

THIMBLE

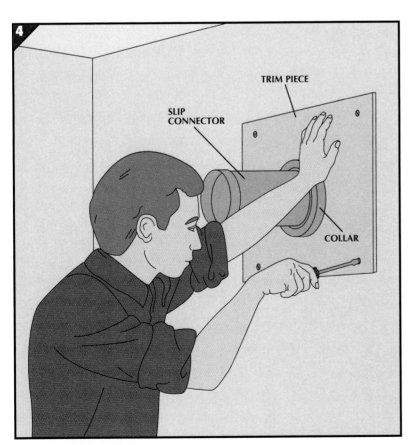

TRIM PIECE

SLIP
CONNECTOR

COLLAR

4. Disguising the thimble.

The thimble is covered by a slip connector, collar, and trim piece. The flange on the slip connector is held in place by the collar; the trim piece fits over the collar's flange.

◆ Slide the trim piece around the thimble and mark the location of the trim's predrilled holes on the wall. Remove the trim, drill a hole into the wall at each mark, and drive in lead anchors.

◆ Fit the slip connector over the thimble, slide the collar over the slip connector to cover the thimble, and fasten the trim piece to the wall by driving $1\frac{1}{2}$-inch No. 8 wood screws into the anchors *(left)*.

◆ Fasten the collar to the thimble by drilling three pilot holes through both pieces and driving a $\frac{3}{4}$-inch No. 8 sheet-metal screw into each hole.

◆ Fasten a stovepipe to the connector as on page 41, Step 5.

Factory-built fireplaces combine the look of a traditional fireplace with the efficiency of a wood stove. But the quality of these appliances varies widely. Select an efficient fireplace that is certified as low-emission by the EPA.

Situating the Appliance: Prefabricated fireplaces, often called "zero-clearance," have built-in shielding that allows them to be placed directly against a stud wall. As such, they can be faced with plywood, paneling, wallboard, brick, stone, or tile veneer (*page 103*). Because of the close tolerances, follow the manufacturer's installation instructions closely.

Extending 18 inches in front of and to each side of the fireplace, a hearth of ceramic, stone, or other fireproof material is required to protect the floor from embers (*pages 100-102*). The fireplace can be elevated on a platform, if desired. Make a frame of 2-by-4s spaced at intervals of 16 inches or less with a $\frac{5}{8}$-inch plywood top.

Venting the Unit: This type of fireplace must be connected to the insulated flue pipe that is sold with the unit. The pipe ordinarily requires a 2-inch clearance from combustibles and is installed in much the same way as a flue for a wood stove (*pages 39-42*). Try to locate the fireplace so the flue can run straight up to the roof without hitting any joists, wires, or other obstacles.

 CAUTION When cutting through walls, ceilings, or roofing, take precautions against releasing lead and asbestos particles into the air (page 36).

 TOOLS

Screwdriver
Electronic stud finder
Compass

Electric drill
Compass saw
Saber saw
Plumb bob
Hammer
Pliers

 **MATERIALS**

Hose clamps
Fiberglass insulation blanket
Duct tape
Sheet-metal screws ($\frac{1}{2}$" No. 8)

Insulated flue pipe
2 x 4s
Common nails ($1\frac{1}{2}$", $3\frac{1}{2}$")
Wallboard and installation materials
Molding

SAFETY TIPS

Put on goggles when driving nails and when operating power tools. Wear gloves, long sleeves, goggles, and a dust mask when installing fiberglass insulation.

A prefabricated fireplace.

The factory-built fireplace at right is a triple-walled box lined with insulation and firebrick. Folding glass doors seal off the firebox from the room, reducing the loss of warm air up the chimney. Air—drawn in through the grille below the firebox—is heated as it circulates in a chamber surrounding the firebox, and flows back into the room through the grille near the top of the unit and the hot-air ducts above the fireplace. Cold-air intake ducts direct outside air into the firebox to feed the fire.

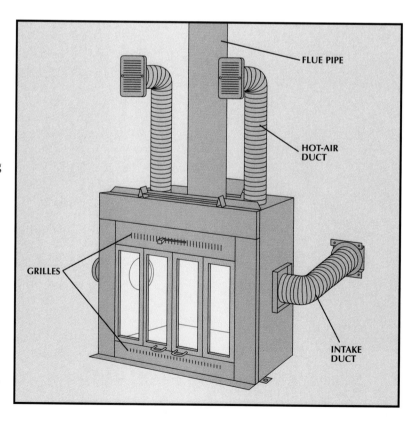

FLUE PIPE

HOT-AIR DUCT

GRILLES

INTAKE DUCT

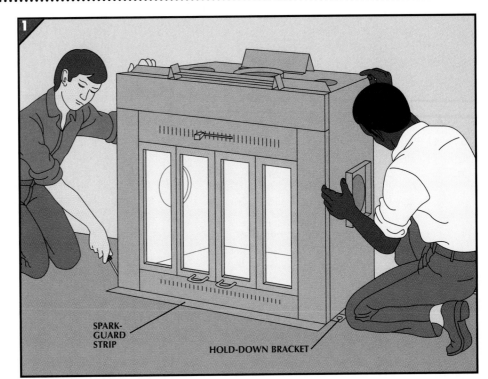

1. Positioning the unit.

◆ Remove a section of baseboard from the exterior wall where you plan to place the unit.

◆ Place the firebox against the wall.

◆ With a stud finder, locate and mark the first pair of studs on each side of the firebox, and center the unit between them.

◆ Slide the metal spark-guard strip under the front of the firebox.

◆ With the screws supplied, anchor the side hold-down brackets to the floor (right).

SPARK-GUARD STRIP

HOLD-DOWN BRACKET

2. Fitting the air-intake ducts.

◆ Make two marks on the wall 18 inches up from the floor, centering the marks between the pairs of studs on either side of the air-duct openings in the firebox.

◆ With a compass, scribe a $4\frac{1}{2}$-inch circle around each mark.

◆ Drill a $\frac{1}{2}$-inch hole within each circle, then cut out the circles with a compass saw or saber saw (left).

◆ Mark the circle on the inside of the exterior wall and cut through the wall with a saber saw or reciprocating saw.

◆ From outside, slide a vent assembly for the air-intake duct into each hole, and attach the assembly to the siding with the screws provided (inset).

3. Installing the cold-air ducts.

◆ Fit one end of the metal air duct on the duct collar on one side of the firebox *(right)*. Secure the connection with a hose clamp.

◆ With a second hose clamp, attach the other end of the duct to the vent assembly installed in Step 2.

◆ Wrap the duct with fiberglass insulation, taping it in place. Install a duct on the other side of the firebox in the same manner.

4. Connecting the flue and hot-air ducts.

◆ Fit a length of insulated flue pipe on the flue collar on the top of the firebox *(left)*.

◆ Attach the pipe to the collar by drilling pilot holes through both pieces and fastening with $\frac{1}{2}$-inch No. 8 sheet-metal screws.

◆ Extend the chimney through the roof as described on pages 39 to 42.

◆ Fasten the hot-air duct collars to the top of the firebox with the L-brackets and screws supplied *(inset)*. Attach each hot-air duct to its collar with a hose clamp.

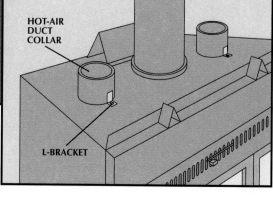

BUILDING STUD WALLS

Framing and covering the walls.

◆ Lay out the enclosure, offsetting the outside edges of the front-wall studs from the front of the stove by the thickness of the wallboard or paneling you will use to cover the walls. Line up the sides of the enclosure with the house wall studs.

◆ Cut 2-by-4 sole plates and nail them to the floor with $3\frac{1}{2}$-inch common nails.

◆ With a plumb bob, align the top plates above the sole plates and nail them to the ceiling joists.

◆ Frame the wall with 2-by-4 studs spaced at 12-inch intervals, toenailing them to the top and bottom plates. Box in the fireplace at the top with a header—two 2-by-4s nailed together —and a jack stud on each side. Make frames to fit the hot-air duct registers 18 inches below the ceiling and pull the ducts up through the frames.

◆ Cover the frame with wallboard or paneling, leaving openings for the hot-air duct registers. Conceal the joints between the wall and fireplace with strips of molding.

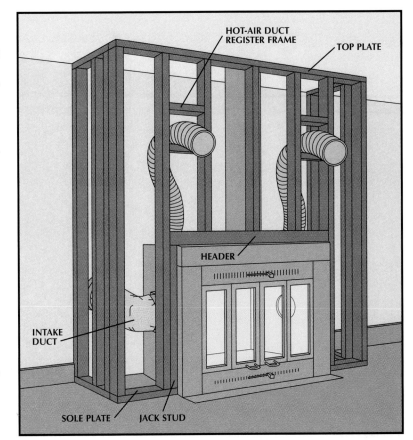

HOT-AIR DUCT REGISTER FRAME

TOP PLATE

HEADER

INTAKE DUCT

SOLE PLATE

JACK STUD

SECURING THE HOT-AIR DUCTS

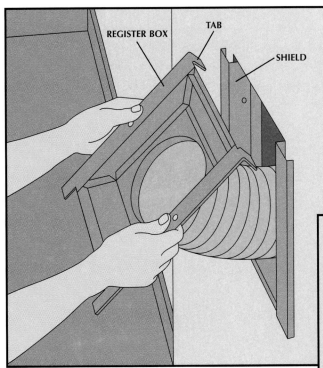

REGISTER BOX

TAB

SHIELD

Mounting the hot-air duct registers.

◆ Fasten the shields to the sides of the duct openings with $1\frac{1}{2}$-inch common nails, leaving a $\frac{1}{8}$-inch gap between the shields and the wall surface.

◆ With hose clamps, connect the ducts to the flanges on the register box.

◆ With pliers, bend the tabs at the top of each register box down and hook them over the shields (left). Fit the boxes in their openings, bend the lower tabs, and hook them under the bottom of the shields.

◆ Screw the register grilles in place, louvers angled downward.

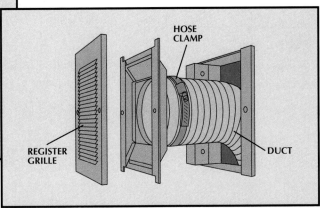

HOSE CLAMP

REGISTER GRILLE

DUCT

3

A Fireplace of Brick and Mortar

The fireplace was once an integral part of domestic life, used for cooking as well as heating. With its smaller, shallower firebox and a separate air intake, the modern version focuses on heating efficiency. This chapter shows you how to build a traditional single-story fireplace from the ground up, from the solid masonry base to the chimney.

Parging the firebox →

Building a Masonry Fireplace

Constructing a masonry fireplace from the ground up is an ambitious project, but careful planning and attention to detail will allow you to build one into an exterior wall with relatively little disturbance to the existing structure.

Strength and Design: A fireplace is basically a freestanding masonry tower, typically weighing about 11 tons. Component parts are linked tightly with mortar, wall ties, and steel rebars. A design that promotes efficient burning is also crucial *(pages 8-11)*. Refer to the chart below and drawings opposite as guides in developing your design. Then consult a professional to finalize the design and ensure that it meets local building codes. You'll need to select the fireplace's finishing materials in advance. Whether you use

brick, stucco, tile, marble, slate, stone, or wood for the facing, hearth, and mantel, the thickness of the materials must be integrated into the design.

Positioning the Fireplace: Ideally a fireplace should be situated near the center of the house so most of the heat it produces will stay inside. But adding such an edifice to an existing house involves major structural disruptions. A more practical alternative is a fireplace built against an exterior wall, located where rerouting of electric wires, plumbing, and ductwork will not be required.

Fireplace location affects the height of the chimney. Codes typically require a chimney to extend 3 feet above the roof and 2 feet above any other structure within 10 feet, including the roof ridge.

Estimating Materials: Before you begin construction, assemble the materials you'll need. To estimate the number of bricks required, calculate the square footage of all the brick surfaces. Multiply this figure by 6.66 and add 5 percent to allow for breakage. For the concrete-block foundation walls, multiply the estimated square footage by 1.125.

You will also need terra-cotta flue liners and firebricks for the firebox. Concrete blocks and standard bricks are set in standard masonry mortar. The firebricks, flue liners, and the inside of the smoke chamber require a special fireplace mortar known as refractory cement.

To estimate the amount of concrete that will be needed for the foundation footing and hearth slab, measure the space in cubic feet each will occupy.

Firebox-opening height	Firebox width	Firebox height	Firebox depth	Fireback width	Fireback height	Damper width	Flue-liner dimensions	Height to header
24"	26"	32"	16"	13"	14"	$8\frac{3}{4}$"	8" x 12"	52"
24"	28"	32"	16"	15"	14"	$8\frac{3}{4}$"	8" x 12"	52"
29"	30"	37"	16"	17"	14"	$8\frac{3}{4}$"	13" x 13"	57"
29"	32"	37"	16"	19"	14"	$8\frac{3}{4}$"	13" x 13"	57"
29"	36"	37"	16"	23"	14"	$8\frac{3}{4}$"	13" x 13"	57"
29"	40"	37"	16"	27"	14"	$8\frac{3}{4}$"	12" x 16"	57"
32"	42"	40"	16"	29"	14"	$8\frac{3}{4}$"	16" x 16"	60"

Fireplace dimensions.

Dimensions that affect fireplace efficiency are listed across the top of this chart. The heights and widths in the first two columns reflect the most common sizes of fireplace openings. For the fireplace to operate at peak efficiency, the dimensions in the next six columns must be proportioned to the size of this opening. The final column gives the header height, which is the height of the opening to be cut through the wall.

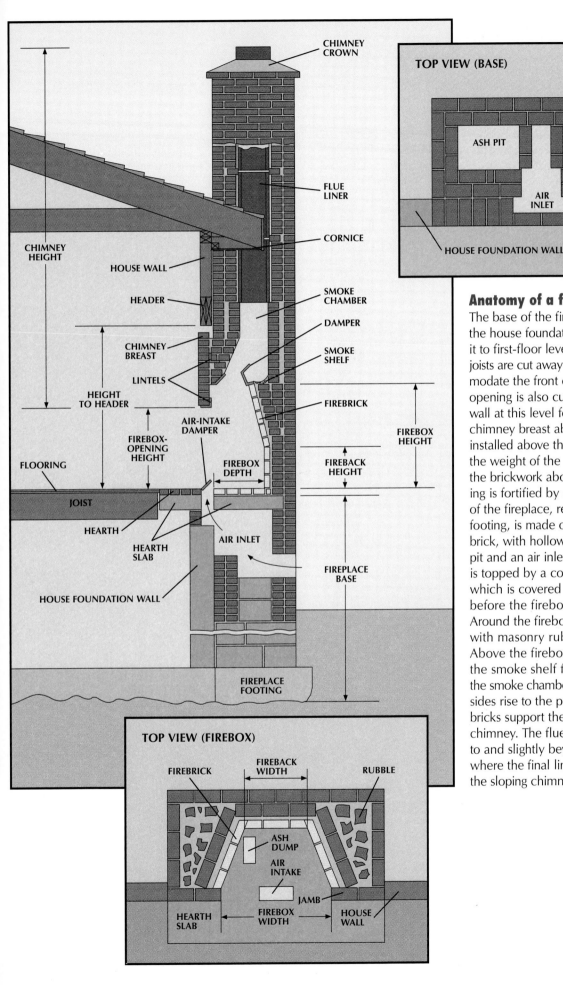

TOP VIEW (BASE)

RUBBLE

ASH PIT

AIR INLET

HOUSE FOUNDATION WALL

CHIMNEY CROWN

FLUE LINER

CORNICE

SMOKE CHAMBER

DAMPER

SMOKE SHELF

FIREBRICK

FIREBOX HEIGHT

FIREBACK HEIGHT

FIREPLACE BASE

HOUSE WALL

HEADER

CHIMNEY BREAST

LINTELS

AIR-INTAKE DAMPER

FIREBOX-OPENING HEIGHT

FIREBOX DEPTH

CHIMNEY HEIGHT

HEIGHT TO HEADER

FLOORING

JOIST

HEARTH

HEARTH SLAB

AIR INLET

HOUSE FOUNDATION WALL

FIREPLACE FOOTING

TOP VIEW (FIREBOX)

FIREBRICK

FIREBACK WIDTH

RUBBLE

ASH DUMP

AIR INTAKE

JAMB

HEARTH SLAB

FIREBOX WIDTH

HOUSE WALL

Anatomy of a fireplace.

The base of the fireplace butts against the house foundation and rises beside it to first-floor level, where the floor joists are cut away and boxed to accommodate the front of the hearth slab. An opening is also cut through the exterior wall at this level for the firebox and the chimney breast above it. A header is installed above this opening to support the weight of the house above, while the brickwork above the firebox opening is fortified by steel lintels. The base of the fireplace, resting on a concrete footing, is made of concrete block and brick, with hollow sections for an ash pit and an air inlet *(top inset).* The base is topped by a concrete hearth slab, which is covered by a layer of firebrick before the firebox is built atop it. Around the firebox are brick walls filled with masonry rubble *(bottom inset).* Above the firebox, the damper and the smoke shelf form the bottom of the smoke chamber, whose three sloping sides rise to the point where the interior bricks support the first flue liner of the chimney. The flue liners are stacked up to and slightly beyond the chimney top, where the final liner is surrounded by the sloping chimney cap.

Mastering the Fundamentals of Bricklaying

Building a brick fireplace requires that you master basic masonry techniques; the life expectancy of the finished product will be directly proportional to the quality and consistency of your workmanship.

Mortar, Cement, and Concrete: To bond bricks and concrete blocks together, it's best to make your own mortar from separate ingredients. By doing so, you can regulate the size of the batches, preparing only what you can conveniently use. The refractory cement used to anchor firebricks and flue liner sections comes ready to use in 5-gallon pails. To pour concrete slabs, buy premixed dry ingredients—just add water.

Cutting Masonry Units: During the construction of the fireplace, you will have to cut bricks to size *(page 59)*. Blocks may also require cutting, as well as the terra-cotta flue liner *(page 60)*.

Building Patterns: Concrete blocks are laid much like bricks, with $\frac{3}{8}$-inch mortar joints *(opposite)*, but trowel the mortar onto the narrow edges of the block a little at a time. Arrange the units in a pattern that masons term "running bond," with each unit equally overlapping the vertical mortar joint of the two below.

Working at a Height: Scaffolding will be required to build the higher part of the chimney *(page 61)*. The scaffolding can be rented, and most outlets will deliver it to the site. You'll need pliers and wrenches for assembly. Take extra care when working at heights *(page 18)*.

 TOOLS

Mason's trowel	Ball-peen hammer
Mason's line	Circular saw with masonry blade
Mason's level	Pliers
Convex jointer	Wrench
Brick set	Hammer

 **MATERIALS**

Mortar ingredients (Portland cement, masonry sand, hydrated lime)
Bricks
Common nails ($3\frac{1}{2}$")

 SAFETY TIPS

Don gloves, goggles, and a dust mask before cutting masonry or mixing mortar and concrete; wear long sleeves when working with the wet mix. Hard-toed shoes protect feet from dropped bricks or blocks.

MIXING MORTAR

Mortar is composed of Portland cement, masonry sand (not beach sand), hydrated lime, and water, mixed together in specific proportions. Masonry cement—premixed cement and lime—can be substituted for the total amount of cement and lime.

The recipes for the three basic types of mortar are shown in the chart below. Type N is the all-purpose type; Type M is specified for underground applications; and Type S is best for areas subject to seismic activity. The standard recipes for making 1 cubic foot of each type are listed at right.

You can mix mortar in a wheelbarrow using a mortar hoe, but for big jobs, consider renting a power mixer. Start by thoroughly mixing the dry ingredients, then push them to one end of the wheelbarrow. Pour several gallons of water into the other end, then pull the dry materials into the water. Add water and mix until there are no lumps and the mortar has the consistency of soft mush.

Pull the hoe through the mix to create a curved furrow; if its sides don't collapse and the mortar can be shaken off the hoe, the mix is ready. Add dry ingredients if the furrow's sides collapse; add a bit more water if the mortar clings to the hoe when shaken. Test the mixture again, adjusting it once more if necessary.

MORTAR RECIPES

Type	Portland Cement	Hydrated Lime	Sand
M	$2\frac{1}{2}$ gal.	$\frac{1}{2}$ gal.	$7\frac{1}{2}$ gal.
N	$1\frac{1}{4}$ gal.	$1\frac{1}{4}$ gal.	$7\frac{1}{2}$ gal.
S	$2\frac{1}{2}$ gal.	$1\frac{1}{4}$ gal.	$8\frac{3}{4}$ gal.

1. Throwing a line of mortar.
◆ Scoop up enough mortar to half-fill the blade of a mason's trowel, then snap the trowel sharply downward to compact the load.
◆ Set the point of the trowel face up against the end of the last brick laid, then slide the trowel along the top of the course below as you rotate the blade forward 180 degrees *(right)*. A properly loaded trowel will deposit a 1-inch-thick layer of mortar across the top of two or three bricks.

2. Furrowing the mortar.
Immediately after throwing the line of mortar, draw the point of the trowel along the center of the mortar bed *(left)*. This spreads the mortar slightly toward the edges, distributing it evenly for the next course of bricks.

3. Buttering the bricks.
◆ For all bricks except those at the end of the row, scoop up enough mortar to cover one end of the brick with a $\frac{3}{4}$-inch layer of mortar *(right)*.
◆ Spread the mortar with the trowel, using the edge of the trowel to remove any excess that slides onto the face of the brick.

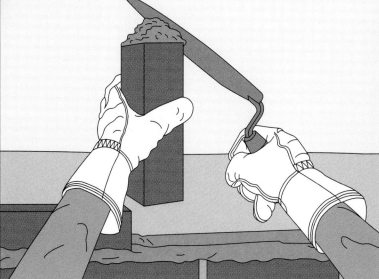

4. Laying the brick.

◆ Place the brick in the bed of mortar, with its buttered end facing the preceding brick *(left)*.

◆ In one motion, force the brick down into the mortar and against the next brick until the vertical and horizontal joints between the bricks are a uniform $\frac{3}{8}$ inch and the face of the brick just touches the mason's line.

◆ Check the wall with a mason's level *(photograph)* every third row to ensure it is staying even.

MASON'S LINE

5. Finishing the joints.

◆ With the edge of the trowel, scrape off any excess mortar *(right, top)*.

◆ After laying several courses, but within an hour, press your thumb against the mortar joint. When the mortar will just hold a thumbprint—firm but not yet hardened—it is time to finish the joints. With a convex jointer, compress the mortar joints, shaping them into concave depressions *(right, bottom)*.

Splitting a brick.
◆ Pencil a cutting line on both edges of the brick, then rest it on the ground in a bed of sand.
◆ With the waste portion facing away from you, place a brick set on the line with the bevel facing the waste portion. Tap it with a ball-peen hammer to score the brick *(right)*.
◆ Score the other cutting line in the same way.
◆ Place the brick set on the scored line and strike it sharply to split the brick.

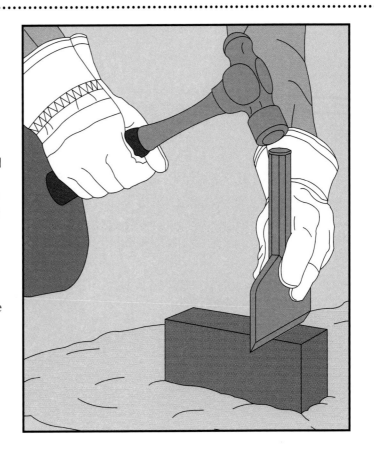

TRICKS OF THE TRADE

Gang-Cutting Bricks

Scoring 6 to 10 bricks at once will ensure uniformity and speed up construction. Line up the bricks on edge and secure them with a pair of bar or pipe clamps as shown, then mark the desired length along the top and bottom edges. Fit a circular saw with a masonry blade and set the cutting depth to about $\frac{1}{8}$ inch. Keeping the blade to the waste side, cut along the marked line. Turn the assembly over to score the other cutting line, then remove the clamps. Split the bricks with a brick set and ball-peen hammer as shown above.

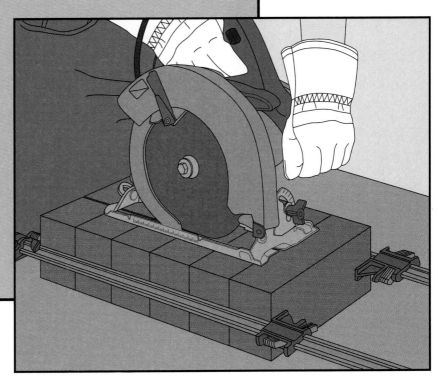

SPLITTING A CONCRETE BLOCK

WEB

Making the cuts.
◆ Mark a cutting line on all four sides of the block. Avoid cutting through a web; if necessary, cut in from both ends of the block instead.
◆ Hold the brick set on the line with its beveled edge toward the waste portion. Tap the brick set lightly with a ball-peen hammer, moving it along the line *(left)*.
◆ Alternate sides of the block, deepening the cut with each pass until the block splits.

TRIMMING A TERRA-COTTA FLUE LINER

Cutting with a circular saw.
◆ Mark a cutting line on all four sides of the liner.
◆ Install a masonry blade on a circular saw and adjust it to cut no more than $\frac{3}{8}$ inch deep.
◆ Start the saw with its blade clear of the liner, then move the blade slowly along the cutting line *(right)*. Stop cutting at the end of that side and turn off the saw.
◆ Repeat on the other three sides then lower the blade another $\frac{3}{8}$ inch and repeat.
◆ Increase the blade depth in $\frac{3}{8}$-inch increments until you have cut through the liner.

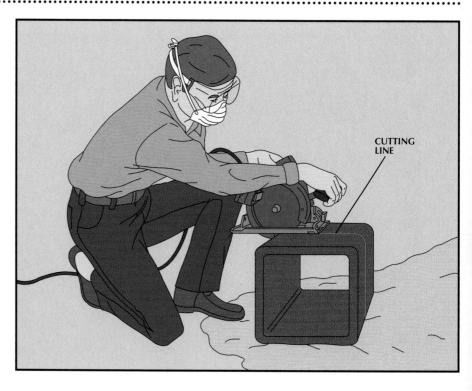

CUTTING LINE

Freestanding scaffolding.
The legs of a modular pipe scaffold are equipped with adjustable base plates that rest on 2-by-12 planks, called sills. The base plates can be elevated individually to level the assembly. The welded frames at each end of the structure incorporate ladders and are held upright by cross braces. Extra end-frame sections can be added on top of the first set to increase the height of the scaffold. Aluminum-framed plywood planks, called walk boards, hook over the tops of the end frames to serve as the working platform. A guardrail is fastened to the end frames on three sides of the scaffold.

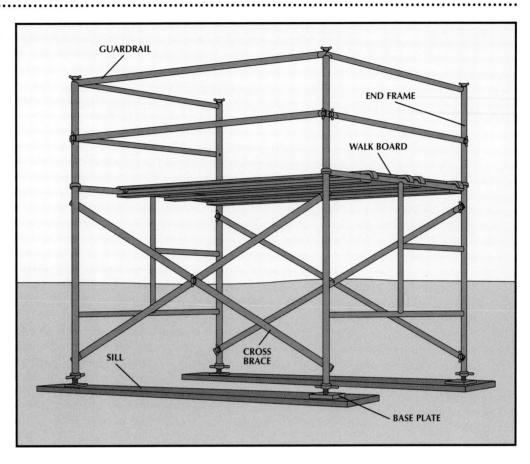

Roof scaffolding.
The mason's roof scaffolding illustrated at left adjusts to any slope and supports walk boards with its pipe frame and cross braces. The frame members that lie on the roof have flat ends that slide under the shingles and are nailed into rafters with $3\frac{1}{2}$-inch common nails. They can also be held in place with the ridge hooks shown on page 18.

Constructing a Base for a Fireplace

The strength and stability of a fireplace depend largely on the base that supports it. Beginning below ground and rising to the level of the firebox, the base extends into the house to support the hearth as well. The guidelines on pages 54 and 55 will help you plan the size of the base in relation to the firebox and chimney.

Cutting into the House: In framing the hearth opening, you will have to cut into the floor joists. If your house has open-web or I-beam joists—manufactured members fastened together with metal connectors or in the shape of an "I"—do not cut them; get the advice of a professional before starting the job.

Casting the Footing: Most building codes dictate that the footing for the base be poured below the frost level; some require that it be the same depth as the house footing. For a one-story exterior chimney, a typical concrete footing is 12 inches thick, extending 6 inches beyond the outer walls of the base. In many cases you can pour the footing without building wooden forms, but the walls of a deep excavation may need shoring.

Ash pit and Air Inlet: The ash pit can be any size and can be located anywhere in the base. The air inlet, however, must measure 55 square inches or more at all points; the vent to the outside can be located anywhere on the base's outer walls, but the opening into the firebox must be located at the front and center of the firebox floor. You will need metal fittings—available at fireplace-supply stores—for these openings. If the vent opening is an odd size, you can cover it with fine-mesh screen.

⚠️ **CAUTION** Before cutting into your house, see page 36 for advice on dealing with lead or asbestos in wall and floor materials.

⚠️ **CAUTION** Before excavating, establish the locations of underground obstacles such as utility lines.

TOOLS

Tape measure
Circular saw
Mason's level
Hammer
Carpenter's square
Maul
Shovel

Hacksaw
Electric drill
Tamper
Wood float
Plumb bob
Chalk line
Mason's trowel
Mason's line
Tin snips

MATERIALS

Masonry nail
String
Stakes
Rebar ($\frac{1}{2}$")
Tie wire
Concrete mix
Mortar ingredients
(Portland cement, masonry sand, hydrated lime)

Polyethylene sheeting
Lumber for story pole
Semisolid concrete
blocks (12", 16")
Metal mesh
Bricks
Wall ties
Steel lintels
Ash-pit door
Air-inlet vent
Plywood ($\frac{1}{2}$")

SAFETY TIPS

Goggles and a dust mask provide protection when you are removing wall materials and cutting brick or block. Wear gloves when working with mortar, and hard-toed shoes while handling bricks and blocks.

Outlining the openings.

◆ Turn off the power to electrical circuits in the work area in case you drill into wires.
◆ Mark the dimensions of the firebox opening *(chart, page 54)* on the interior wall in the desired location.
◆ Add a second outline around the first that is 16 inches wider on each side and 28 inches higher. This delineates the wall opening for the brick jambs and chimney breast.
◆ Mark the opening for the hearth on the floor as wide as the wall opening and 16 inches out from the wall.
◆ At each corner of the larger outline, drill a hole through the wall and floor. Make the floor holes large enough to accept a saber saw blade.
◆ Mark lines on the floor 2 inches outside the hearth outline, defining the placement of a hardwood frame that will be laid when the hearth is in place.

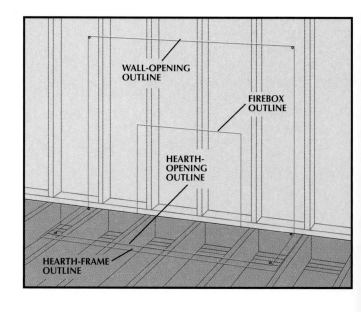

WALL-OPENING OUTLINE

FIREBOX OUTLINE

HEARTH-OPENING OUTLINE

HEARTH-FRAME OUTLINE

1. Laying out the footing.

◆ Guided by the drilled holes, outline the hearth opening on the exterior wall, then cut out the first 18 inches of siding and sheathing above the foundation with a circular saw.

◆ With a level, draw a plumb line on the house foundation 6 inches outside each side of the wall opening.

◆ Drive a masonry nail into the foundation along one of the plumb lines and tie a string to the nail.

◆ Hold a carpenter's square against the nail and stretch out a string perpendicular to the wall.

◆ Fasten the string to a stake about 8 inches beyond the planned front of the footing and pound the stake into the ground *(left)*.

◆ Stake a second identical string at the opposite plumb line.

◆ Set up a third set of stakes and string for the front edge of the footing that crosses the first two strings at 90 degrees. Check that the layout is square by measuring the diagonals between opposite corners—they should be equal *(inset)*. If not, adjust the location of the third string and recheck the diagonals.

2. Leveling the site.

◆ Excavate to the planned depth of the base plus the depth of the footing. Remove the strings and stakes.

◆ With a hacksaw, cut five 16-inch lengths of $\frac{1}{2}$-inch steel reinforcing bar (rebar). Near each corner of the excavation and at the center, drive a length 4 inches into the ground.

◆ Lay a level across adjacent rebar pegs and adjust the depth of the pegs so all their tops are level, making sure each protrudes at least 1 foot above the ground *(right)*.

◆ Smooth and level the bottom of the pit, tamping the dirt firmly around each peg.

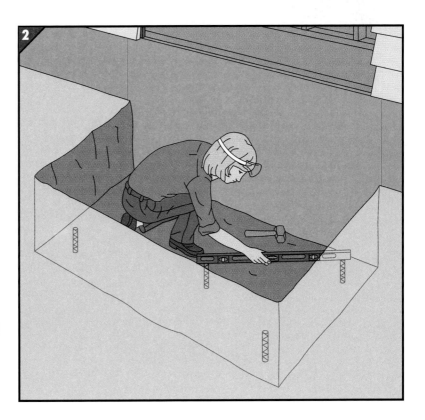

3. Positioning the rebars.

◆ Cut enough lengths of rebar to span the width and length of the pit at intervals of 8 inches.

◆ Lay the rebars across the pit, supported on pieces of brick or rebar bolsters *(photograph)*, forming a grid.

◆ Wire the rods together at each intersection *(right)*; also wire the rods to the pegs.

◆ Pour concrete into the pit to the tops of the pegs. Smooth and level the footing with a wood float. Cover the concrete with polyethylene sheeting to keep it damp, and allow it to cure for a week.

BUILDING THE BASE WITH BLOCK AND BRICK

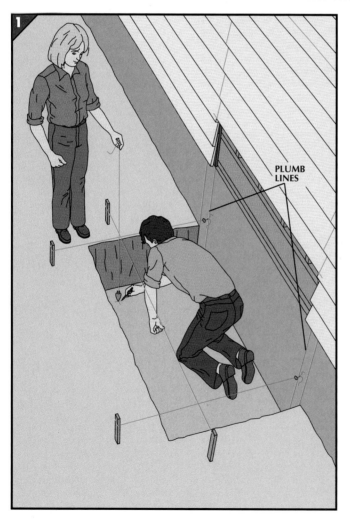

PLUMB LINES

1. Outlining the base.

◆ With a level, draw plumb lines down the house foundation from the edges of the wall opening to the footing.

◆ Lay out the base on the footing, using stakes and strings in the same way you did for the footing *(page 63, Step 1)*.

◆ At each outer corner of the outline, drop a plumb bob to the footing, and have a helper mark the corners on the concrete *(left)*.

◆ Snap three chalk lines across the footing to connect the corners.

2. Laying the blocks.

◆ To keep the heights of the courses consistent, make a story pole: On a piece of lumber, make a mark every $8\frac{3}{8}$ inches—the height of a block plus a $\frac{3}{8}$-inch mortar joint.

◆ At one front corner of the base outline, throw a mortar bed for a 16-inch semisolid corner block and set the block in place. Tap it with the trowel handle until its top is level with the first mark on the story pole.

◆ Butter the end of a second corner block and lay it against the first, squaring them with a carpenter's square; then check it with the story pole.

◆ Complete the corner—called a lead—by laying a 12-inch corner block atop the first two, aligning its top with the second mark on the story pole *(right)*.

◆ Lay a second corner lead at the other end of the base outline and check that both corners are level and plumb.

◆ Fasten a mason's line to the corners at the first mortar joint and lay a row of blocks between them *(inset)*.

◆ Set a row of blocks against the house foundation and between the front and back corner leads, then fill in between the rows with more blocks, spreading mortar on their sides and ends.

◆ Checking that the courses are consistent, level, and plumb, continue building the base, stopping about 8 inches below ground level.

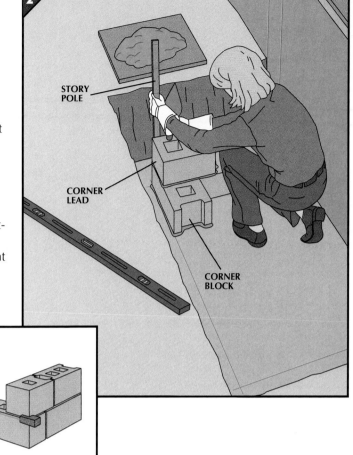

STORY POLE

CORNER LEAD

CORNER BLOCK

3. Laying the first brick courses.

◆ Mark the other side of the story pole to accommodate bricks rather than blocks.

◆ Lay a strip of metal mesh two bricks wide around the edge of the blocks.

◆ Lay a corner lead two bricks wide and three courses high at each outer corner of the base, adding wall ties to link the front and back bricks in each course and checking the courses with the story pole.

◆ With a mason's level, check that the bricks on both sides of each corner are level, plumb, and straight *(left)*.

◆ Lay three courses of bricks between the corners, working all around the base. Then fill in the core with a course of concrete blocks mortared together.

◆ Lay one more double-course of bricks around the perimeter of the base and backfill the pit around the base to ground level *(inset)*.

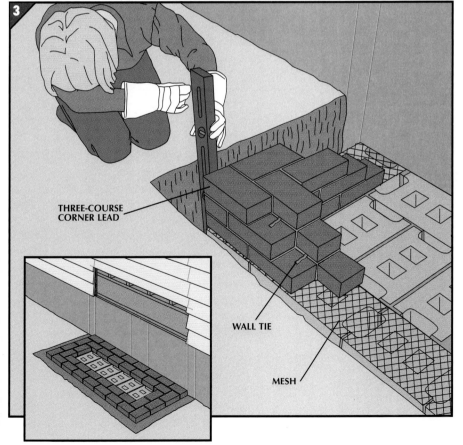

THREE-COURSE CORNER LEAD

WALL TIE

MESH

4. Locating the air inlet and ash pit.

◆ Measure to the middle of the wall opening, and mark points $6\frac{1}{2}$ inches on each side of the midpoint.

◆ From each mark, draw a plumb line on the house foundation down to the brick wall. Extend the lines across the top of the bricks.

◆ Establish two partition walls in the base by laying a row of bricks end to end across the base at each guideline.

◆ Line the bottom of the ash pit and air inlet with a course of mortared bricks laid flat *(left)*.

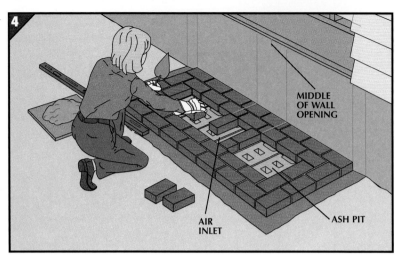

MIDDLE OF WALL OPENING

AIR INLET

ASH PIT

5. Framing the openings for the inlet and ash pit.

◆ Continue raising the four sides of the base and the partition walls. For the ash-pit door, leave a 1-foot-wide gap beginning one brick course above ground level; for the air-inlet vent, leave a gap as wide as the passageway between the two partitions, starting three brick courses above ground level.

◆ After laying six brick courses, cut two $2\frac{1}{2}$-by-3-by-$\frac{3}{16}$ steel lintels 6 inches longer than the ash-pit door opening and another two 6 inches longer than the air inlet vent opening.

◆ Lay the lintels back to back across each opening *(right)*, centering their backs over the joint between the double wall of bricks.

◆ Apply a very thin layer of mortar on the lintels and lay a course of bricks on them. The sparing use of mortar will maintain the height of the brick course.

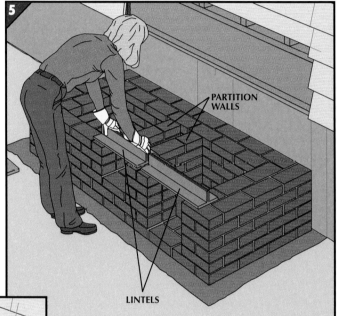

PARTITION WALLS

LINTELS

6. Finishing the base.

◆ Mortar the ash-pit door and the air-inlet vent in place, adding extra mortar to fill any gaps around the edges.

◆ Build up the outer brick and partition walls until they are level with the top of the house foundation *(left)*. As you build up the wall along the house, leave an opening between the guidelines that mark the partition walls for the air inlet.

◆ Fill the hollow section to the left of the air inlet with mortared blocks or mortar and rubble.

◆ Once the mortar is hard enough to hold a thumbprint, finish the joints *(page 58)*.

AIR-INLET VENT

ASH-PIT DOOR

Extending the Base into the House

Once the base of the fireplace reaches the height of the proposed hearth slab, you can open the house wall and floor and frame them.

Framing the Floor Opening: The method in which the floor opening is framed depends on whether the floor joists run perpendicular or parallel to the wall where the fireplace will be located *(below and page 68, Step 2)*. Before cutting into any floor joists, brace them with temporary supports.

Opening the Wall: If joists run perpendicular to the wall, before cutting the wall opening, build a shoring wall to support the ceiling joists above the opening *(page 68, Step 3)*. Where joists run parallel to the wall, forgo the shoring and simply remove the wall covering and studs *(page 69)*. Frame the opening with a header and studs *(page 70)*.

Casting the Hearth Slab: The hearth slab on these pages is poured to a depth designed to accept a brick veneer; if the finish on the hearth will be any other material thinner than brick, such as marble, slate, or tile, you will have to make the slab thicker.

⚠ **CAUTION** *Wall and floor materials sometimes contain asbestos or lead. Before cutting into your house, see page 36 for advice on dealing with these hazards.*

TOOLS		**MATERIALS**			**SAFETY TIPS**

TOOLS		**MATERIALS**		
Utility knife		Joist hangers	Sheet metal	
Chisel		($1\frac{1}{2}$", 3")	Motor oil	
Hammer	Wrench	1×1s, 1×4s	Framing connector	Rebar ($\frac{1}{2}$")
Saber saw	Hacksaw	2×2s, 2×4s	nails	Tie wire
Handsaw	Mason's	4×4s	Laminated veneer	Concrete mix
Carpenter's	trowel	Joist lumber	lumber	Polyethylene
level	Mason's level	Plywood	Bricks	
Hand stapler	Electric drill	($\frac{1}{4}$", $\frac{1}{2}$")	Mortar ingredients	
Circular saw	Tin snips	Shims	(Portland cement,	
Pry bar	Wood float	Common nails	hydrated lime,	
		($3\frac{1}{2}$")	masonry sand)	

SAFETY TIPS

Wear goggles when using power tools or driving nails. Don gloves, goggles, and a dust mask when removing wall materials. Put on gloves to work with wet or dry mortar or concrete; add a dust mask when mixing these products, and hard-toed shoes as protection against dropped bricks.

CUTTING THROUGH THE WALL AND FLOOR

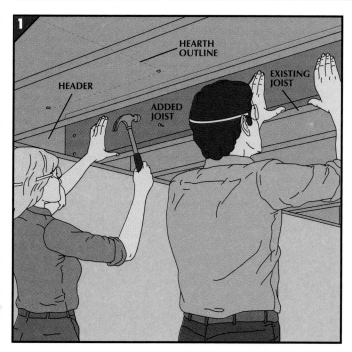

HEARTH OUTLINE

HEADER

ADDED JOIST

EXISTING JOIST

1. Reinforcing the floor joists.
◆ Working below the floor, outline the hearth opening, guided by the holes you drilled.
◆ For joists perpendicular to the wall, cut two joist-size boards, and attach them to the joists outside each side of the opening with $3\frac{1}{2}$-inch common nails every 12 inches in a W pattern *(left)*.
◆ Wedge a 4-by-4 support post under each joist between the double joists, 18 inches beyond the front of the planned hearth.
◆ Cut through the supported joists 3 inches beyond the front of the hearth. Pry the waste piece free from the header atop the foundation.

◆ If the joists run parallel to the wall, wedge two 4-by-4 support posts under the joist closest to the wall, positioning them 18 inches beyond each side of the hearth opening.
◆ Cut a section from the joist closest to the wall equal to the width of the planned hearth, plus 3 inches on each side.
◆ Install a new full-length double joist flush with the front of the hearth opening; secure it with 3-inch joist hangers.

2. Installing a header.

◆ For joists that are perpendicular to the wall, assemble a header—made of two lengths of joist lumber fastened together with $3\frac{1}{2}$-inch common nails—to fit between the reinforced joists.

◆ Fasten 3-inch joist hangers to both ends of the new header with framing connector nails.

◆ With a helper, raise the header into position, butting against the cut joists, and secure the joist hangers to the reinforced joists.

◆ Fasten joist hangers to the cut joists *(right)*, and nail the hangers to the header.

For joists parallel to the wall, install a header along each side of the planned hearth opening: Toenail one end of each header to the joist atop the foundation wall with $3\frac{1}{2}$-inch common nails, and fasten the other end to the new doubled joist with a 3-inch joist hanger. Secure the ends of the cut joists to the header with $1\frac{1}{2}$-inch joist hangers, then proceed to Step 4, omitting the shoring wall in Step 3.

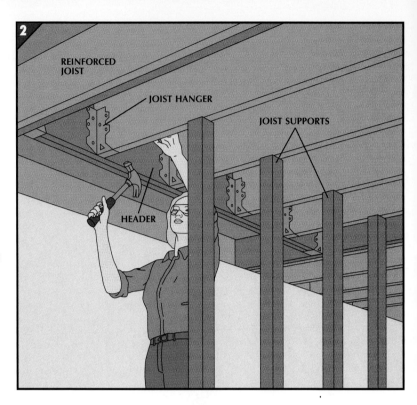

3. Building a shoring wall.

Where the floor and ceiling joists run perpendicular to the wall opening, build a 2-by-4 stud wall to support the house above the wall you will be cutting through. Make it 1 foot longer than the opening and cut the studs $4\frac{1}{2}$ inches shorter than the floor-to-ceiling height.

◆ Fasten the studs to the top and bottom plates at 24-inch intervals with $3\frac{1}{2}$-inch nails.

◆ Brace the framework with two 1-by-4s nailed diagonally to opposite corners.

◆ Staple strips of carpet to the top of the top plate.

◆ Cut a strip of $\frac{1}{4}$-inch plywood and position it in front of the opening about 4 feet from the wall and, with a helper, lift the shoring wall onto the strip.

◆ While the helper holds the wall plumb, tap shims between the strip and the sole plate at each stud so the wall presses firmly against the ceiling *(above)*.

4. Cutting out the wall opening.

◆ Turn off the power to electrical circuits in the work area in case you cut into wires.

◆ Place a sheet of $\frac{1}{2}$-inch plywood on the fireplace base as a working platform.

◆ With a circular saw set to the combined depth of the siding and sheathing, cut through the wall along the outline *(left)*.

◆ Pry the sheathing within the outline away from the studs.

◆ When you are not working on the fireplace, deter thieves and keep the weather out by nailing a sheet of plywood across the wall opening and covering the plywood with plastic.

5. Cutting the studs.

◆ Working inside, remove a section of wall covering surrounding the opening; cut from floor to ceiling and to the first studs that are at least $3\frac{1}{2}$ inches outside the wall opening. If the opening is wider than 72 inches, remove the wall covering to the first studs that are at least 5 inches outside of the opening.

◆ Remove any exposed insulation, then cut each stud $11\frac{1}{2}$ inches above the top of the opening.

◆ Pull and twist the studs away from the sole plate *(right)*, forming cripple studs above the opening; then cut through the sole plate at the edges of the fireplace opening and pry the plate up.

CRIPPLE STUDS

SOLE PLATE

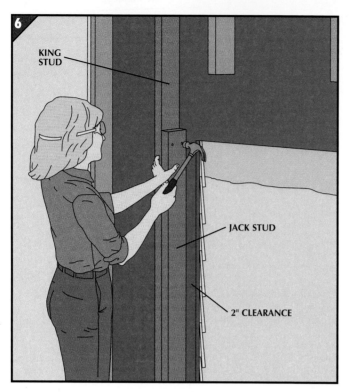

KING STUD

JACK STUD

2" CLEARANCE

6. Installing jack studs.

◆ If there are no existing wall studs within 5 inches of the opening, use $3\frac{1}{2}$-inch nails to toenail an extra wall stud—called a king stud—to the top and sole plates. When the opening is narrower than 72 inches, toenail the king studs $3\frac{1}{2}$ inches from each edge of the opening. If it is wider than 72 inches, toenail the king studs 5 inches from each side of the opening.

◆ For each king stud $3\frac{1}{2}$ inches from an edge of the opening, cut a jack stud 2 inches longer than the height of the opening. For a king stud 5 inches from the edge, cut two jack studs.

◆ Nail a jack stud to the inside surface of each king stud with 3-inch common nails spaced 4 to 6 inches apart *(left)*. Fasten the second jack stud, if there is one, to the first. In either case, leave 2 inches of clearance between the jack studs and the wall opening.

CRIPPLE STUD

HEADER

7. Securing the header.

◆ Assemble a header by nailing together two pieces of laminated veneer lumber (LVL) of the size required by code to span the opening between the king studs. Fasten the pieces together with $3\frac{1}{2}$-inch nails, driven in a zigzag pattern into both sides at 10-inch intervals.

◆ With a helper, set the header atop the jack studs.

◆ Drive $3\frac{1}{2}$-inch nails through the king studs into the header *(above)*. Toenail the header to the jack studs, and toenail the cripple studs above the opening to the top of the header.

◆ Take down the shoring wall.

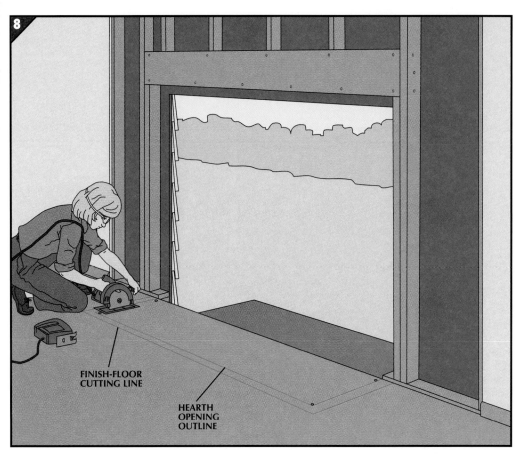

8. Opening the floor.

◆ Insert a saber saw blade into each hole in the corner of the hearth opening outline and make a cut a few inches long. Finish cutting the outline of the hearth opening with a circular saw, with the blade set to the depth of the finish floor and subfloor *(left)*. Pry up the floor and subfloor.

◆ Set the circular saw depth to the thickness of the finish floor and cut along the outline of the finish floor, leaving the subfloor intact. Then, clean up the corners of the cut with a chisel.

FINISH-FLOOR CUTTING LINE

HEARTH OPENING OUTLINE

9. Removing the header and sill.

◆ Working outside with a handsaw, cut the joist atop the sill plate flush with the edges of the opening. Knock out the waste piece.

◆ Cut through the sill plate *(right)*. With a wrench, remove the anchor bolt nuts securing the waste piece to the house foundation and lift it off. If the nuts are stuck, cut the sill plate on both sides of each anchor bolt and wedge up the sections with a pry bar.

◆ With a hacksaw, cut off the anchor bolts flush with the top of the foundation.

JOIST

ANCHOR BOLT

SILL PLATE

PREPARING FOR THE HEARTH SLAB

1. Raising the base to floor level.

◆ Cover the house foundation wall with two courses of bricks, laying those opposite the air inlet in line with the foundation and the others across it *(right)*.

◆ Lay two more double-width courses of bricks around the perimeter of the base and on the partition walls. Add rubble to the solid-core section to the left of the air inlet to bring it level with the brickwork.

◆ Complete the base by laying three single-width courses of bricks around the three outer walls, creating a lip for the sheet-metal cover that will underlay the hearth slab *(inset)*. Start these walls by laying corner leads, then check their tops with a mason's level to be sure they are level with the finish floor inside before filling in between them.

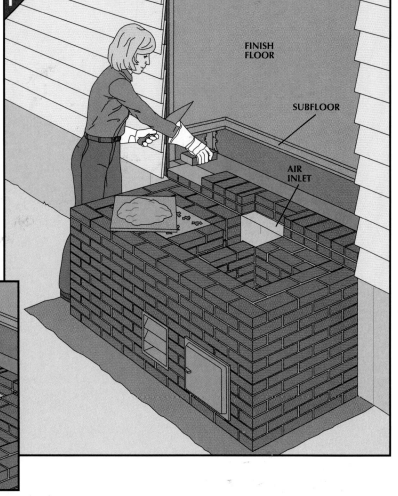

FINISH FLOOR

SUBFLOOR

AIR INLET

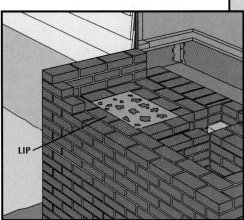

LIP

2. Marking the template.

◆ Cut a sheet of $\frac{1}{4}$-inch plywood to fit flush against the three single-width walls above the lip and overlap the midpoint of the house foundation.

◆ Draw lines on the plywood to establish the location of the firebox *(pages 54-55)*.

◆ Set the ash-dump door within the firebox outline, positioning it close to the rear of the firebox. Outline the vertical flange on the template *(right)*.

◆ Center the air-inlet damper along the front of the template and outline it.

◆ Drill a $\frac{1}{2}$-inch hole through the template within the ash-dump door outline, then cut out both outlines with a saber saw.

◆ Cut a sheet of 24-gauge metal to the same size as the template. Trace and cut matching openings in the metal.

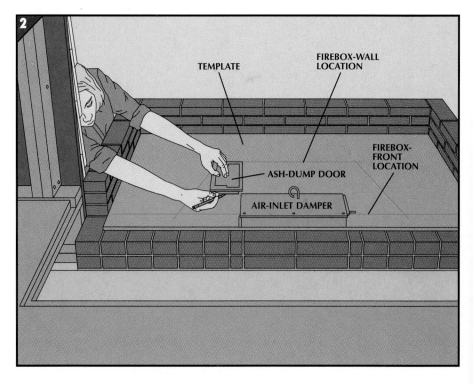

TEMPLATE

FIREBOX-WALL LOCATION

FIREBOX-FRONT LOCATION

ASH-DUMP DOOR

AIR-INLET DAMPER

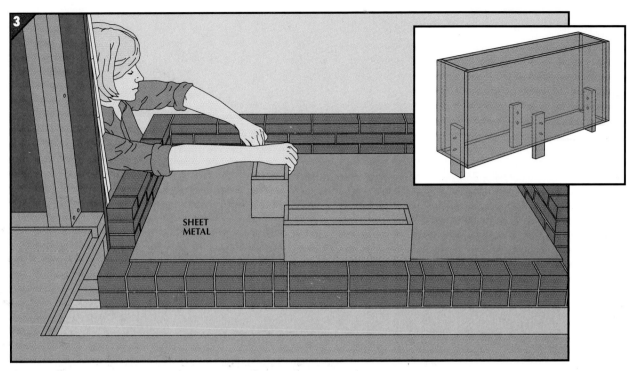

SHEET METAL

3. Making concrete forms.

◆ Construct an 8-inch-high box form from $\frac{1}{2}$-inch plywood so its inside dimensions match the ash-dump hole opening in the sheet-metal cover. Make a simi-lar form for the air-inlet notch.

◆ Nail a 1-by-2-inch strip, 6 inches long, to each inside face of each form so the strips extend 2 to 3 inches past the bottom edges *(inset)*.

◆ Position the forms over their openings, slipping the strips in until the boxes are flush against the metal.

◆ Grease the outside surfaces of the forms with motor oil.

POURING THE CONCRETE

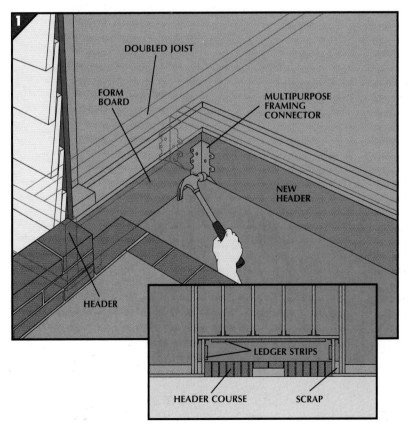

DOUBLED JOIST

FORM BOARD

MULTIPURPOSE FRAMING CONNECTOR

NEW HEADER

HEADER

LEDGER STRIPS

HEADER COURSE   SCRAP

1. Preparing the opening.

◆ If the floor joists run perpendicular to the wall, and the joists you doubled in Step 1, page 67, are not flush with the sides of the hearth opening, cut two form boards to fit between the new header and the header atop the foundation wall.

◆ To the ends of each form board, nail multipur-pose framing connectors facing the opening.

◆ Align the boards' inside faces with the edge of the opening and nail the connectors to the new header *(left)*.

◆ Wedge scrap lumber between the form boards and the doubled joist on top of the sill; toenail the form boards to the scrap.

◆ To support the floor of the form, cut 2-by-2-inch ledger strips about 8 inches shorter than the form boards. Nail the ledger strips to the form boards and the new header, aligning the top of the strips with the top of the brick header course *(inset)*.

Where the floor joists run parallel to the wall, cut and nail ledger strips to the new joists and new headers framing the hearth opening.

2. Making a floor for the form.

◆ Cut a piece of $\frac{1}{2}$-inch plywood to fit within the hearth opening against the form boards, header, and brickwork of the base.

◆ Cut a notch in the plywood so it will butt against the edge of the sheet metal and set it in place on the brick header course and ledger strips *(left)*.

◆ Support the plywood from below with 4-by-4 posts, placing one at each corner and two in the center.

3. Positioning the rebars.

◆ Lay a grid of $\frac{1}{2}$-inch rebars on the sheet-metal cover and plywood floor at 8-inch intervals.

◆ Support the rebar 2 inches above the plywood and the sheet metal with brick fragments or rebar bolsters *(page 64, Step 3)*.

◆ Fasten the bars together at intersection points with wire.

4. Pouring the slab.

◆ Prepare concrete according to the directions on the bag, and pour it level with the bottom of the top mortar joint in the back wall of the base.

◆ Smooth and level the concrete with a wood float, taking care not to displace the forms framing the openings *(left)*.

◆ Cover the concrete with a sheet of polyethylene and allow it to cure for seven days.

◆ Remove the box forms and 4-by-4 supports.

Erecting the Firebox and Smoke Chamber

The firebox, smoke shelf, and smoke chamber, though distinct from their surrounding exterior masonry, are built with it—almost course by course—as a unit.

Planning the Courses: Each course—whether of standard brick or firebrick—is first laid without mortar in a trial run called dry bonding. With dry bonding, you can adjust mortar joint widths and cut bricks to exact sizes before you cement them in place. This is especially important when building the fireback, whose corner bricks must be cut at compound angles *(page 80)*.

Corbeling: To make the smoke chamber angle inward from the damper to the flue, offset each course of bricks up to 1 inch over the edge of the course below it, creating a stepped effect called corbeling. A corbeled smoke chamber is sturdier if it is two courses thick; strengthen such a wall by laying an occasional brick perpendicular to the bricks below.

Sealing: The back of the firebox and the inside of the smoke chamber are covered with a layer of mortar $\frac{1}{4}$ to $\frac{1}{2}$ inch thick. This coating—known as parging—seals and insulates the firebox and smooths the path of the smoke. Parging mortar should be prepared drier than normal so that it will adhere to the bricks better; even so, a good deal of the mortar will fall off the bricks as you apply it. On corbeled bricks, apply the mortar in two coats—one to fill in the stepped offsets, the other to build up a smooth surface.

Strengthening: The space between the outer walls and the firebox and smoke chamber should be filled in with rubble—whole bricks and concrete blocks for large spaces, broken bits of masonry for tight corners and small spaces. Stabilize the rubble with plenty of mortar; tie it to adjacent walls with wall ties, set crosswise and embedded in the mortar joints of the rubble and walls.

TOOLS

Chalk line	Straightedge
Mason's trowel	Brick set
Mason's level	Ball-peen
Carpenter's square	hammer
	Tape measure
	Circular saw

MATERIALS

Bricks	Fireplace mortar
Firebricks	Heavy paper
Wall ties	Plywood ($\frac{1}{4}$")
Mortar ingredients	Air-inlet damper
(Portland cement,	Ash-dump door
masonry sand,	Damper
hydrated lime)	Steel lintels
	Fiberglass insulation
	Plastic sheeting

SAFETY TIPS

Wear gloves when working with mortar; add goggles and a dust mask when mixing it. Goggles are required when operating power tools or cutting bricks; don hard-toed shoes to protect yourself when working with bricks. Wear gloves, long sleeves, goggles, and a dust mask to handle fiberglass insulation.

FIREBRICKS THAT TAKE THE HEAT

The firebox of a fireplace is not only subjected to extreme heat from fire, but must withstand a repeating cycle of heating and cooling. Standard bricks would fracture in these conditions. Firebricks, also known as refractory bricks, are designed to survive the rigors of a firebox. Usually available only in beige and red, firebricks can be handled, cut, and laid the same way as standard bricks, but fireplace mortar instead of regular mortar is used to cement them in place.

1. Laying the firebox floor.

◆ Mark the front of the firebox by snapping a chalk line across the wall opening in line with the front of the air inlet. Then dry-lay two standard bricks end to end at each side of the opening, flush with the chalk line. These bricks form the first course of the fireplace jambs. Mortar the jamb bricks in place.

◆ Fill in between the jambs and the air inlet with dry-laid firebricks, leaving $\frac{1}{8}$ inch between units for mortar joints.

◆ Set a row of firebricks behind the first, offsetting mortar joints and overlapping the jamb bricks by one-half brick.

◆ Continue placing firebricks in rows to within 1 or 2 inches of the back edge of the concrete slab. Cut bricks as necessary to fit around the ash-dump opening *(page 59)*.

◆ When you are satisfied with the arrangement and spacing of the firebricks, remove them from the slab and set them aside in position. Spread a $\frac{1}{2}$-inch bed of fireplace mortar on the slab and lay the firebricks in place with $\frac{1}{8}$-inch mortar joints between them. Check each row with a level; tamp down bricks that sit too high. Avoid shifting the bricks as you go.

◆ When the mortar is thumbprint-hard, level the joints.

◆ Insert the air-inlet damper and ash-dump door in their openings *(inset)*.

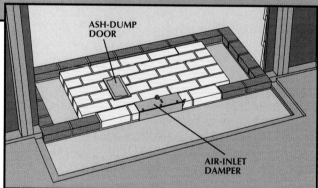

2. Locating the firebox walls.

◆ Mark a center line on the firebox floor midway between the edges of the slab. Then, referring to the chart on page 54, measure from the back edge of the air-inlet damper and mark the fireback on the center line.

◆ With a carpenter's square, draw perpendicular lines on each side of the center line, half the width of the fireback *(left)*.

◆ With a straightedge, connect the ends of the fireback line to the top corners of the jamb bricks *(dashed line)*.

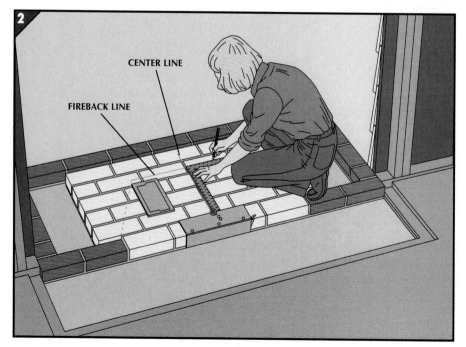

BEVEL

3. Laying the firebox walls.

◆ Starting flush against the top corners of the jamb bricks, place unmortared firebricks on edge $\frac{1}{4}$ inch apart, aligned with the firebox outline.

◆ With a brick set and ball-peen hammer, bevel the bricks at the back corners of the firebox so they align with the side wall.

◆ Remove the bricks, cover the floor of the firebox with heavy paper to catch any mortar spills, and bond the bricks in place with fireplace mortar.

◆ Prepare the next course, offsetting mortar joints, then mortar them in place *(above)*.

◆ Once you've laid three courses of bricks, check the walls for plumb and level.

4. Parging the firebox.

With a mason's trowel, seal the firebricks by coating the outside of the firebox walls with a layer of fireplace mortar $\frac{1}{4}$ inch thick. Spread the mortar from the bottom up *(right)*.

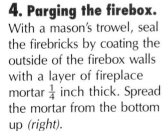

FIREPLACE MORTAR

BACKING THE WALLS

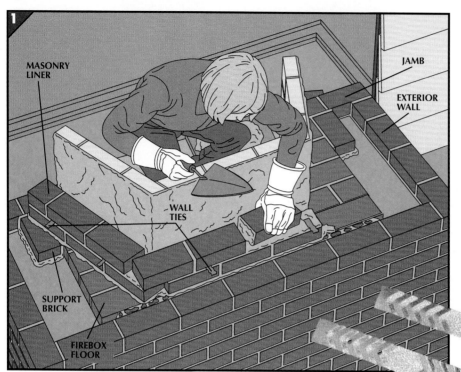

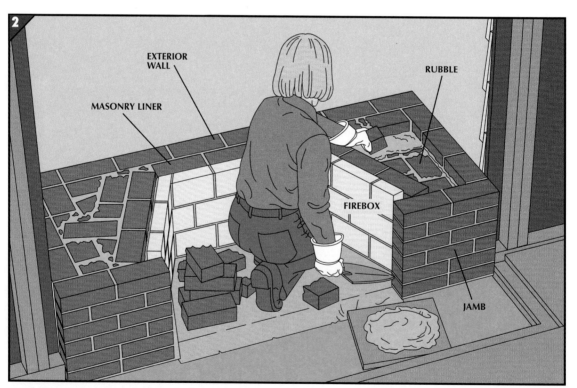

1. Building the masonry liner.
◆ Lay a standard brick as a support in each corner formed by the brick jambs and the firebox floor.
◆ Lay the first course of the liner walls parallel to the firebox walls, starting at the back of the jambs. Leave a gap of $\frac{1}{2}$ to 1 inch between the liner and the firebox walls so the back wall of the liner is almost flush with the exterior wall of the fireplace. Embed two wall ties *(photograph)* on each wall of the liner.
◆ Build up the liner *(left)*, the exterior walls of the fireplace, and the jambs to the height of the firebox walls. Offset mortar joints and add two wall ties to each wall of the liner in every course of bricks.

2. Filling in the cavities with rubble.
Pack pieces of brick and concrete blocks between the masonry liner and the exterior walls of the fireplace, fitting the pieces around the wall ties set in Step 1. Add plenty of mortar to ensure that all the space is filled.

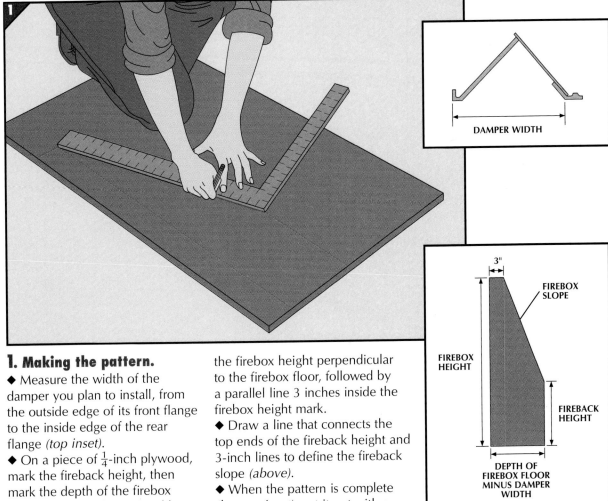

1. Making the pattern.

◆ Measure the width of the damper you plan to install, from the outside edge of its front flange to the inside edge of the rear flange *(top inset)*.

◆ On a piece of $\frac{1}{4}$-inch plywood, mark the fireback height, then mark the depth of the firebox floor, minus the damper width.

◆ With a carpenter's square, mark the firebox height perpendicular to the firebox floor, followed by a parallel line 3 inches inside the firebox height mark.

◆ Draw a line that connects the top ends of the fireback height and 3-inch lines to define the fireback slope *(above)*.

◆ When the pattern is complete *(bottom inset)*, cut it out with a circular saw.

DAMPER WIDTH

3"

FIREBOX SLOPE

FIREBOX HEIGHT

FIREBACK HEIGHT

DEPTH OF FIREBOX FLOOR MINUS DAMPER WIDTH

PATTERN

2. Building the sloping walls.

◆ Place a thick line of mortar on the firebricks in the center portion of the fireback.

◆ Set a firebrick in the mortar, centering it over a mortar joint in the course below.

◆ Holding the pattern with the fireback height edge against the fireback wall, tip the brick forward so it rests flush on the sloped edge *(left)*. The mortar joint will be compressed to about $\frac{1}{4}$ inch thick in front and wider at the back.

◆ Steady the brick for several seconds to let the mortar bond, then lay the remaining bricks in the course of the back wall the same way.

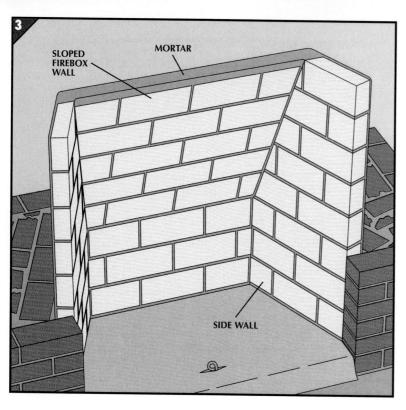

3. Completing the firebox walls.

◆ As you raise the sloping firebox wall, build the side walls as well, cutting the corner bricks of the side walls to match the side walls. Because of the forward slope, the mortar joints of the side walls will be slightly above those of the back wall. The end bricks in each course of the sloping wall will rest on the end bricks of the side walls.

◆ Once the firebox walls attain their full height, parge the outside surfaces with fireplace mortar *(page 77, Step 4)*.

◆ At the top of the firebox, run an extra-thick layer of mortar across the top of the sloped wall to bring it to the level of the side walls *(left)*.

SCULPTING THE SMOKE SHELF

1. Building up the smoke shelf.

◆ Assemble a scaffold as a stable work platform *(page 61)*.

◆ As you raise the walls, corbel the back of the inner masonry liner to follow the sloped firebox wall, leaving about 1 inch between the two elements. Fill the space behind the liner with mortared rubble *(page 78)*. As soon as the space between the liner and the rear wall is large enough to accommodate a full brick, resume building a double thickness of brick up the rear wall *(right)*.

◆ Raise the jambs to the height of the firebox opening, anchoring every few courses to the rubble with wall ties.

◆ Raise the liner to within 2 or 3 inches of the top of the firebox, setting the final bricks perpendicular to the sloped wall, mortaring this final course against the firebox to seal off the space between the firebox and the liner.

◆ Raise the doubled rear wall one course above the height of the firebox.

◆ Build up the exterior side walls partway, so the sides step down from the exterior rear wall to the top of the jamb. The steps enable you to interlock the bricks of the side walls with the bricks of the chimney breast *(page 82, Step 3)*.

2. Parging the smoke shelf.
◆ Spread a layer of standard mortar $\frac{1}{4}$ to $\frac{1}{2}$ inch thick between the top of the fireback and the exterior rear wall *(right)*.
◆ Trowel the mortar into a smooth, slightly concave surface that covers the top course of the masonry liner and curves up against the exterior wall.
◆ Build up the rubble behind the jambs and the stepped-down exterior side walls so it is level with the bricks around the smoke shelf.

SETTING THE DAMPER AND LINTELS

1. Installing the damper.
◆ Set the damper on top of the firebox with its hinged plate to the rear and its front flange flush with the front edges of the firebox walls.
◆ Position the damper so its back flange rests securely on the top of the fireback.
◆ Lift each end of the damper and wrap the side flange with fiberglass insulation *(left)*; this will allow the metal to expand without cracking the masonry.

As you build up the bricks around the damper, open the damper plate from time to time to be sure the plate clears the structure.

2. Setting the lintels.
◆ Position a steel lintel—its L shape facing forward—across the jambs against the front corners of the firebox walls, overlapping the bricks at least 3 inches at each end.
◆ Set a second lintel—its L shape facing to the rear—on the bricks one course above the front flange of the damper. Align the lintel with the front corners of the firebox wall *(right)*.
◆ Wrap fiberglass insulation around the ends of both lintels.

3. Raising the chimney breast.

◆ Apply a very thin layer of mortar on the lintel spanning the fireplace opening and lay a course of bricks on it *(right)*. The sparing use of mortar will maintain the height of the brick courses.

◆ As you lay additional courses across the chimney breast, alternately overlap the end bricks of the breast and the exterior wall, creating a continuous running-bond pattern that wraps the front corners of the fireplace.

◆ Step down the bricks of the side walls *(page 80, Step 1)* toward the back wall.

◆ Raise the chimney breast to within 2 inches of the header at the top of the wall opening. When laying the last few courses, you will have to work alternately inside and outside the house to bring the walls together.

BUILDING THE SMOKE CHAMBER

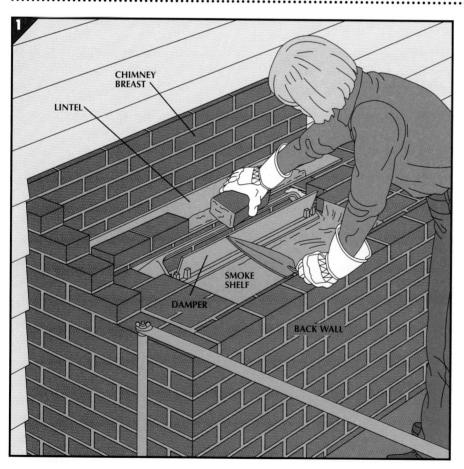

1. Laying the first course.

◆ Working from the scaffold outside the house, set a row of bricks across the lintel above the damper.

◆ Continue the course by setting bricks along the walls on both sides of the smoke shelf (perpendicular to the ones already there) and across the inner course of the back wall.

◆ Drape a sheet of plastic or heavy paper over the damper and smoke shelf to protect them from falling mortar.

CHIMNEY BREAST

FRONT WALL

PLASTIC SHEET

2. Corbeling the walls.

◆ Lay a second course of bricks around the damper and smoke shelf. Corbel the front wall about 1 inch toward the damper *(left)*; keep the side and back walls vertical.

◆ Lay a third course, this time corbeling both the front and the side walls, and keeping the back wall vertical. In the doubled side walls, orient an occasional brick perpendicular to the others, linking the two layers of brick.

◆ When the third course is completed, fill in the cavity between the corbeled front wall and the chimney breast with rubble and mortar.

3. Parging the smoke chamber.

◆ Parge all interior surfaces of the smoke chamber with standard mortar *(above)*. For the sections of corbeled bricks, apply the mortar in two layers. The first coat will fill in all stepped edges, while the second will create a smooth surface.

4. Raising the smoke chamber.

◆ Continue to raise the walls of the smoke chamber, parging the interior surfaces every two or three courses.

◆ When the distance between the front and back wall is 2 inches larger than the flue liner, stop corbeling the front wall and make subsequent courses vertical *(right)*. At this point, stop doubling the smoke-chamber walls and start building in single courses, continuing to corbel the side walls so as to narrow the chamber opening to the size of the flue liner.

5. Completing the smoke chamber.

◆ As the opening at the top of the smoke chamber approaches the dimensions of the flue liner, measure the opening after each new course *(above)*.

◆ Adjust the amount of side-wall and front-wall corbeling on the last course so the smoke cham-

ber's inside dimensions are equal to those of the flue liner.

◆ Build up the exterior walls of the fireplace to the height of the chimney breast. Fill in the space between the exterior walls and the smoke chamber with mortared rubble.

A Fireplace that Amplifies Heat

Building a circulating fireplace involves relatively simple modifications of the design for a conventional fireplace, but its heating efficiency can be as much as 30 percent greater.

Dimensions: The firebox of a circulating fireplace is deeper than a conventional one, and its side walls are more nearly perpendicular to the fireback. A typical design has an opening 36 inches wide and 18 inches deep with a fireback 28 inches wide and 9 inches high. To accommodate the heat chamber behind the firebox, build the foundation 12 inches deeper and 8 inches wider than the minimum required by code. Build the base described on page 86, or construct one with a hearth slab *(pages 72-74)*.

Building the Fireplace: Employ the same methods as for a conventional fireplace *(pages 62-71)* but use the dimensions above; omit the air inlet and ash pit, and stop the base one course of bricks above the finish floor *(pages 86-89)*. When the firebox is completed, build the chimney *(pages 90-99)*.

Hardware: Electric fans controlled by a thermostat located directly across the room draw air into the heat chamber. Determine the wiring path for the thermostat in your preliminary planning. Unless you are skilled in electrical work, have a professional do the wiring. The fans, thermostat, grilles, and combustion-air damper are available in kit form through fireplace supply stores. For maximum efficiency, fit the fireplace with glass doors.

 TOOLS

Mason's trowel
Hacksaw
Brick set
Ball-peen
 hammer
Caulking gun

 MATERIALS

Bricks
Firebricks
Mortar ingredients
 (Portland cement,
 masonry sand,
 hydrated lime)
Fireplace mortar
Air-duct pipes
Steel lintels
Combustion-air
 damper
Damper
Fiberglass insulation
Air-intake fans and
 thermostat
Air-exit vent grilles
Chimney-rated
 caulk

SAFETY TIPS

Wear gloves when working with mortar; add goggles and a dust mask when mixing it. Put on hard-toed shoes to prevent injury from dropped or falling bricks, and wear goggles when cutting bricks.

A circulating fireplace.

Circulating fireplaces are designed to trap the heat they produce, then move the air into the room through a multipartitioned chamber behind the firebox. Excepting the grilles that cover the intake and exit vents, this type of fireplace is outwardly indistinguishable from a conventional one. The inner workings, however, are quite different *(right)*. The heat chamber behind the firebox is a maze of brickwork, divided in two by a pillar of bricks. Each half is further partitioned into an upper and lower half by a divider shelf. On each side of the center divider, the chamber contains a matching set of four baffles. Air is drawn into the baffled chambers by fans atop the air-intake shafts *(blue arrows)*, then flows through the upper and lower chambers and leaves by the air-exit vents *(orange arrows)*. A combustion-air damper in the floor of the firebox feeds outside air to the fire.

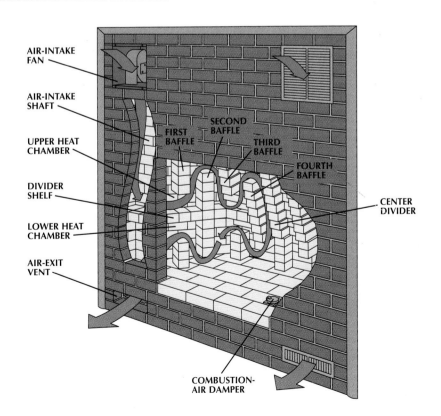

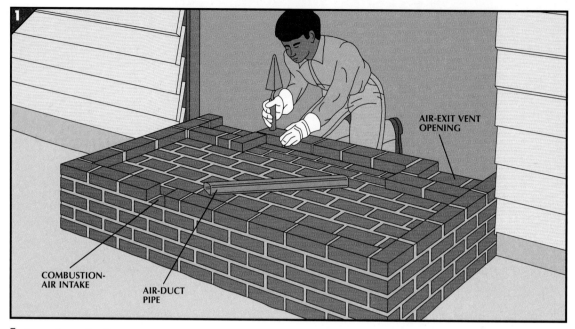

1. Locating the lower vents.
◆ Lay a course of bricks around the perimeter of the base, leaving three openings for air passageways: Three brick lengths from one side of the outer wall, leave one opening 4 inches wide for the combustion-air intake; leave two openings 10 inches wide against the house wall for air-exit vents, framing them with bricks to form a 10-by-4-inch space *(above)*.
◆ Lay a 32-inch-long air-duct pipe in the combustion-air intake opening, its outer end flush with the outer face of the foundation wall, leaving a space at the inner end of the pipe.
◆ Fill in the remaining area of the base with mortared bricks.

2. Completing the base.
◆ Bridge the air-exit vents with steel lintels, and set a second air-duct pipe atop the first one *(right)*.
◆ Lay a second course of bricks on the base.
◆ With mortar, parge over the air-duct pipes to secure them in place *(inset)*.
◆ Lay the first course of fireplace jambs and the firebox floor as you would for a conventional fireplace *(page 76, Step 1)*, except instead of leaving openings for the ash dump or air inlet, leave space for the combustion-air damper at the ends of the air-duct pipes. Install the damper in the floor. Fill the space between the firebox floor and the outer walls with rubble.
◆ Lay out the first two courses of the firebox walls *(page 77, Step 3)*. Parge the outside walls with fireplace mortar, then build up the jambs to the same height.

3. Beginning the heat-chamber walls.

◆ Lay the first two courses of each heat-chamber wall as you would an inner masonry liner *(page 78, Step 1)*, but start the side walls 4 inches back from the jambs to leave room for the air shafts behind the air-exit vents.

◆ Orient bricks at 90 degrees to the course to form headers for the center divider and the first and third baffles on each side of the divider *(above)*. Cut the bricks to fit against the firebox walls.

◆ Mortar the ends of the headers to the firebox walls.

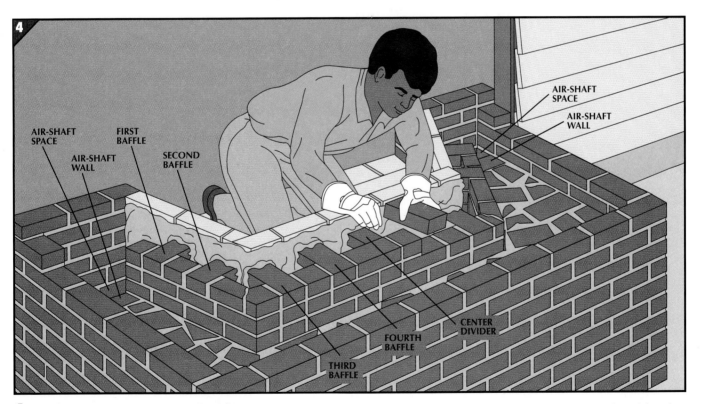

4. Finishing the lower heat chamber.

◆ Lay the third course of the heat-chamber walls, including headers for the center divider and all four baffles on each side *(above)*.

◆ Lay two courses of the sloped firebox walls *(page 79)*.

◆ Lay the next two courses of the heat-chamber walls, with headers at the center divider and at the second and fourth baffles on each side, and corbeling the bricks of the back heat-chamber wall and its baffles so they parallel the firebox wall.

◆ Build the exterior walls, the jambs, and the air-shaft walls to the height of the heat-chamber walls, then fill the area between the air-shaft and exterior walls with rubble and mortar.

5. Building the divider shelf.

◆ Lay the sixth course of the heat-chamber walls perpendicular to the course below, forming a header that butts against the firebox wall *(right)*. Leave a brick-wide air space on each side of the center divider; and cover the air shafts by cantilevering bricks across the opening, mortaring the ends against the jambs.

◆ Finish building and parging the walls of the firebox.

6. Building the upper heat chamber.

The upper heat chamber is built much like the lower one, but with eight courses rather than five. For the first two courses, build only the second and fourth baffles. With the third and fourth courses, include all the baffles *(above)*. For the fifth, sixth, seventh, and eighth courses, lay only the first and third baffles. Include a center divider in each course. Corbel the bricks to parallel the firebox.

◆ Finish the chamber by laying a final course with all the bricks oriented to touch the fireback, leaving a 4-inch space at the top of the air shafts *(inset)*.

◆ Build the exterior fireplace walls and the air-shaft walls two courses higher than the firebox walls; fill the space between the air-shaft and exterior walls with rubble and mortar.

◆ Build the jambs up to the planned height of the firebox opening.

◆ Parge the smoke shelf with standard mortar *(page 81, Step 2)*.

7. Building the chimney breast.

◆ Install the damper and a lintel across the opening, wrapping their ends in fiberglass insulation *(page 81, Steps 1-2)*.

◆ Apply a very thin layer of mortar along the lintel and lay a course of bricks across the lintel and the tops of the jambs *(right)*. Continue building the breast—leaving space behind it for the air shaft—until it reaches the height of the firebox.

◆ Begin to form the smoke chamber, filling the space between the smoke-chamber walls and the exterior walls with brick rubble and mortar as you go *(pages 82-83)*.

8. Installing the air-intake fans.

◆ Spread a layer of mortar $\frac{1}{2}$ to 1 inch thick at the air-intake shaft openings. Set the fan-housing boxes in the mortar, lining up the front of each box with the chimney breast *(left)*.

◆ Wire the fans and the thermostat or have an electrician wire them.

◆ Continue building the chimney breast around the boxes, stopping 2 inches below the bottom of the header that frames the wall opening.

◆ Apply mortar in the gaps around the air-exit vents.

◆ Finish building the smoke chamber and exterior walls, filling the space between them with brick rubble and mortar *(page 84, Steps 4-5)*.

◆ When the mortar has set, seal any gaps around the front of each fan box with chimney-rated caulk and screw the grilles to the boxes.

Fashioning a Sturdy Chimney

Raising a chimney along a house wall requires careful planning and execution. If your home is sided with wood, vinyl, or aluminum, you will need to cut a channel up the wall and through the roof overhang to provide a flat surface for the tower *(below)*. The chimney will have to fit neatly into the gap, with metal flashing where it adjoins the roof. The gradual taper from the firebox to the chimney can be achieved with one or two sloping shoulders, which can be finished with brick, slate, or flagstone.

As you raise the chimney, maintain the 1-inch air space between the flue liner and the inside walls of the tower. This space insulates the flue to keep it hot and encourage a strong draft.

Anchoring the Chimney: For maximum stability, tie the chimney to the house at 16-inch intervals. If your home is sided with brick, remove a brick from the house wall every 6 courses and lay two chimney bricks in the opening perpendicular to the chimney. If the siding is wood, vinyl or aluminum, use wall ties *(page 95)*.

⚠️ **CAUTION** *Wall and roof materials sometimes contain lead or asbestos. Before cutting into your house, see page 36 for advice on dealing with these hazards.*

 TOOLS

Tape measure
Level
Straightedge
Carpenter's square
Plumb bob
Sliding bevel
Circular saw
Saber saw
Handsaw
Prybar
Hammer
Utility knife with
   hooked blade
Tin snips
Mason's trowel
Brick set
Ball-peen hammer
Caulking gun

 MATERIALS

Lumber for
   rafter blocks
Common nails
   (3", $3\frac{1}{2}$")
Flashing metal
Roofing nails ($1\frac{1}{2}$")
Fireplace mortar
Clay flue liners
Bricks
Mortar ingredients
   (Portland cement,
   masonry sand,
   hydrated lime)
Wall ties
Silicone caulk

 SAFETY TIPS

Wear gloves to cut and handle sheet metal, and goggles to operate power tools or to cut bricks. Don gloves when working with mortar; add goggles and a dust mask to mix it. Put on hard-toed shoes to prevent injury from dropped or falling bricks.

CUTTING A CHANNEL IN THE WALL

EXTERIOR WALL   AIR SPACE   INTERIOR WALL

FLUE LINER

RUBBLE

1. Outlining the chimney on the wall.
◆ Find the center of the smoke-chamber wall flanking the house. Measure from this point on both sides to a distance equal to one-half the planned width of the chimney—including the width of the flue liner, a 1-inch air space on each side, and the width of the two walls of bricks plus the rubble-filled space between the walls *(inset)*.
◆ Holding a level vertically at each mark, draw a line up the wall from the top of the bricks to the bottom of the roof overhang *(left)*.

2. Plotting the chimney shoulders.

◆ Establish the slope of the shoulders by measuring the horizontal distance from each width line to the nearest edge of the fireplace.

◆ On each side, measure this same distance up the width line; with a straightedge, draw a line that joins this point and the edge of the fireplace *(above)*.

◆ With a circular saw, cut through the siding along the vertical lines, then cut and pry off the siding between the vertical cuts to expose the sheathing.

3. Marking the eaves.

◆ With a carpenter's square, mark lines across the soffit 1 inch outside the cuts on the siding *(left)*.

◆ Extend the lines across the fascia.

4. Cutting the soffit.

With a saber saw cut through the soffit along the marked lines *(left)*. Pry the waste piece free.

5. Cutting the roof opening.

◆ Establish the location of the top corners of the roof opening by hanging a plumb bob from the underside of the roof sheathing, aligning the bob with the points where the cuts in the soffit and the wall meet. At each corner, mark the string's position on the sheathing, and drive a nail up through the sheathing at each mark.

◆ Outline the roof opening by drawing lines between the nail tips and the marked lines on the fascia *(inset)*.

◆ Using a utility knife with a hooked blade, cut away the roofing material and pull any nails within the outline. With a circular saw, cut through the sheathing along the outline *(right)* and remove the sheathing.

SHEATHING

6. Cutting the fascia and rafters.

◆ With a circular saw, cut through the fascia along the marked lines *(left)*. If the saw is obstructed by roofing at the edges of the opening, complete the cuts with a handsaw.

◆ Cut off any rafters that project into the opening flush with the upper edge of the opening.

◆ Frame the opening and seal off the attic by toenailing wood blocks with $3\frac{1}{2}$-inch common nails between the cut ends of the rafters and the ceiling joists, and between the upper edge of the opening and the fascia. Ensure that the outside face of the boards is flush with the opening.

FLASHING AROUND THE OPENING

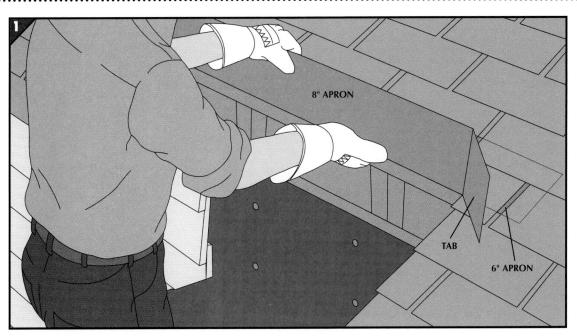

1. Fitting the up-roof flashing.

◆ Cut a piece of flashing metal 14 inches wide and 12 inches longer than the roof opening. Fold the flashing lengthwise 6 inches from one edge, forming 6-inch and 8-inch aprons. With tin snips, make a 6-inch cut along the fold at each end.

◆ Bend the 8-inch apron at the end of each cut, forming tabs 6 inches long.

◆ Wedge the 6-inch apron under the shingles, removing any nails that are in the way, so the 8-inch apron is flush with the upper edge of the roof opening *(above)*.

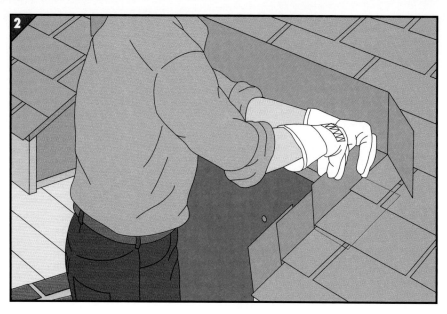

2. Layering the side flashing.

◆ Cut pieces of flashing 7 inches square, then fold each piece in half at 90 degrees.

◆ Slip a piece under the first shingle at one lower corner of the roof opening so its outside edge is flush with the fascia.

◆ Lift the next shingle above and drive a $1\frac{1}{2}$-inch roofing nail through the first shingle and the piece of flashing.

◆ Slip a second piece of flashing behind the first so its outside edge aligns with the lower edge of the next shingle. Nail the flashing to the roof.

◆ Continue fastening flashing until you reach the upper edge of the roof opening *(left)*, then repeat on the other side.

BEGINNING THE FLUE

1. Starting the flue liner.

◆ Spread $\frac{1}{2}$ inch of fireplace mortar around the rim of the smoke chamber and set the first section of flue liner in the mortar *(above)*.

◆ Align the inside rim of the flue liner with the opening in the smoke chamber, compressing the mortar to a thickness of $\frac{1}{4}$ inch.

◆ With a level, check the liner for plumb. Then reach down inside the liner with a trowel and remove any extruded mortar.

2. Starting the chimney walls.

◆ Start building the outer wall of the chimney by laying a course of bricks on the smoke chamber flush against the house sheathing. Align the sides of the wall with the cut siding. Line up the front of the wall with the front of the fireplace base.

◆ Raise the outer walls to the height of the smoke chamber.

◆ Fill the space between the outer walls and the smoke-chamber walls with rubble and mortar *(left)*.

3. Raising the chimney walls.

◆ Build the inner wall 3 courses high, leaving a 1-inch space between the bricks and the flue liner *(right)*.

◆ Raise the outer wall to the same height as the inner one; fill the space between the walls with mortar and rubble.

◆ Continue raising the walls. Every sixth course, anchor the outer wall to the house by pressing a wall tie into the mortar and fastening it to a stud in the house wall with 3-inch common nails *(inset)*.

◆ Stop building when the walls are less than one course from the top of the flue liner.

4. Starting the shoulders.

◆ Establish guidelines for the shoulders by holding a brick against the sheathing on one side of the chimney so the top of the brick is flush against the cut in the siding. Mark a line on the sheathing along the bottom of the brick and extend the line from the top of the smoke chamber to the outer wall of the chimney. Repeat on the other side of the chimney.

◆ On each side of the chimney, lay a wall of bricks against the sheathing between the chimney and the guideline, offsetting the mortar joints and ending each course with a brick beveled flush with the line *(left)*.

5. Laying the front shoulders.

◆ Measure the height and length of the shoulder and transfer the marks to the front face of the chimney and smoke chamber. Drive a nail into mortar joints at each mark, and stretch a string between the nails.

◆ Build a shoulder along the front of the chimney, offsetting mortar joints between successive courses and beveling bricks flush with the string line *(right)*.

◆ Fill the space between the two shoulders with rubble and mortar; cover the top of this fill with a smooth layer of mortar.

◆ Repeat on the other side of the chimney.

6. Capping the shoulders.

Starting at the corner between the chimney and the sheathing, lay bricks on the mortar layer *(left)*. Stagger the mortar joints between adjacent rows and bevel the first and last bricks of each row flush with the edges of the chimney and fireplace wall.

Alternatively, mortar slate or flagstone to the shoulders.

RAISING THE CHIMNEY

1. Measuring for counterflashing.

As you raise the chimney to roof level and above, you will need to install a piece of counterflashing along each side of the chimney with every course of bricks.

◆ Determine how many pieces you need by taking two measurements from the top of the chimney's walls: Measure to the top of the fascia at the lower corner of the roof opening; then to roof level at the opening's upper corner *(right)*. Subtract the first measurement from the second and divide the result by 2.6, a figure that represents the combined thickness of a brick and a mortar joint. Round off the result to the next highest number.

◆ Establish the width of each piece by stretching the tape measure along the soffit from the sheathing to the front of the fascia, dividing the result by the number of pieces, and adding 3 inches.

◆ Measure the roof slope with a T-bevel: Place the handle against the blocking in an upper corner, and align the blade with the roof slope.

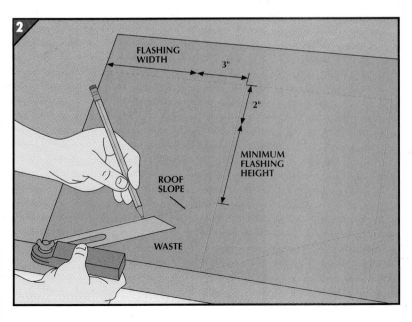

2. Preparing counterflashing.

◆ On a sheet of flashing, mark off the width of the pieces with a carpenter's square, then transfer the roof slope from the T-bevel to the bottom of each section *(left)*.

◆ Establish the height of the pieces by measuring up from the top of the slope line the minimum chimney-flashing height specified by your local building code; add 2 inches to the measurement. For a roof steeper than 6 inches per foot, add another 2.6 inches; when you install the flashing, it will step up every two brick courses per piece instead of one.

◆ With tin snips, trim the flashing along the width, slope, and height lines.

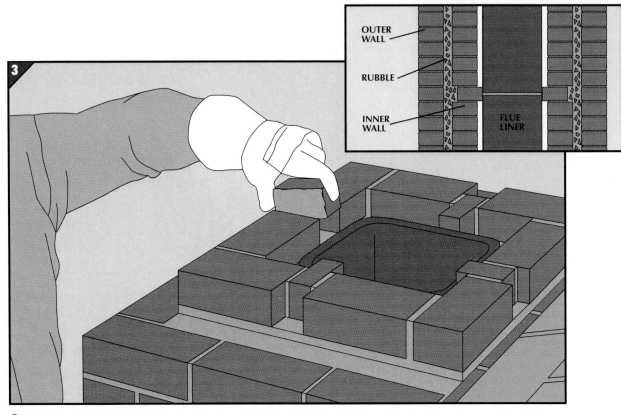

3. Adding flue-liner sections.

◆ For the next course of the chimney, lay the bricks of the inner wall with a brick or brick fragment resting against the flue liner on all four sides *(above)*, then build the outer walls as before. When the chimney is completed, the flue-liner sections will be stabilized by the bricks projecting from the inner walls *(inset)*.

◆ Lay a bed of fireplace mortar on the flue liner and place a second flue liner on top of the first, then reach down into the flue with a soft brush and smooth the mortar joint.

4. Installing the counterflashing.

◆ Raise the chimney until it extends above the roof by an amount equal to the minimum flashing height.

◆ As you lay the bricks for the outer wall, position the first piece of counterflashing over the side flashing, with the sloped bottom flat on the roof and the long edge flush with the eave. Fold the top over the bricks *(right)*, and cover the fold with mortar.

◆ If the next course falls at the top of the flue liner, lay the inner wall as in Step 3, with bricks resting against the liner on all four sides. Install counterflashing as you lay the outer wall, overlapping the previous piece by 3 inches.

◆ Continue raising the chimney, adding a piece of flashing with each course.

5. Finishing the back corner.

◆ Before installing the last piece of flashing, cut a short slit into the up-roof flashing near each end between the tab and the straight section.

◆ Make a vertical fold along the last piece of counterflashing about 1 inch from the short edge, and wrap it around the up-roof corner of the chimney and fold it over the top of the chimney *(right)*.

◆ Wrap the tabs of the up-roof flashing around the counterflashing and fold the top over the chimney wall *(inset)*.

◆ Add another course of bricks to the chimney.

UP-ROOF FLASHING

VERTICAL FOLD

TAB

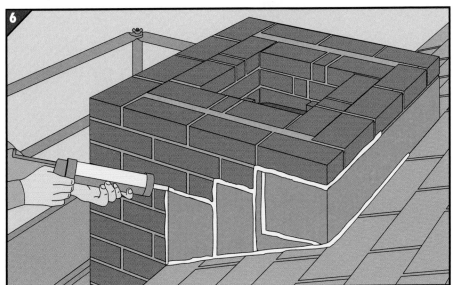

6. Sealing the flashing.

◆ With a caulking gun, run a bead of silicone caulk along all edges of the flashing *(left)*.

◆ Apply caulk along the junction of the chimney and the roof.

◆ Spread a layer of fireplace mortar on the top of the flue liner, then set another liner section in place and smooth the inside joint.

7. Capping the top.

◆ When the chimney is within one course of its final height, corbel the final course of the outer wall so it projects outside the course below by 1 inch *(right)*.

◆ Lay the last course of the inner wall, maintaining the 1-inch air space between the bricks and the flue liner.

◆ Fill in the space between the walls of the last courses with mortar and rubble.

◆ Install a last section of flue liner extending at least 8 inches above the chimney walls.

◆ Make a chimney crown *(page 21)*, leaving at least 4 inches of the liner projecting above the cap *(inset)*.

◆ Remove the protective sheet of plastic from the smoke shelf.

DRIP LEDGE

CHIMNEY CROWN

FLUE LINER

The hearth and facing surrounding a fireplace can be framed simply with brick or embellished with materials like marble, tile, or slate. The first step is to patch the wall adjoining the fireplace with wallboard, butting it against the brick, flush with the front.

Laying the Hearth: The top surface of the hearth must be level with the firebox floor. One approach is to lay bricks in mortar directly over the concrete hearth slab *(below)*. With thinner materials like tile or fieldstone, the slab will need to be built up with a layer of concrete.

A marble or slate hearth *(page 102)* is installed in one piece cut $\frac{1}{16}$ inch smaller than the exposed portion of the slab to allow for expansion. Unlike brick, a marble or slate hearth is not mortared in place but lies on a dry bed.

Facing the Fireplace: If you wish to leave the brick facing around the firebox bare, cover the seam between the masonry and wall with molding *(page 101)*. Select molding wide enough to be nailed in place, such as $2\frac{1}{2}$-inch window casing.

You can also veneer the brick facing with ceramic tile or tile-sized squares of marble or slate *(page 103)*. Tiles with built-in spacer lugs simplify alignment and spacing.

Mounting a Mantel Shelf: The fireplace can be capped with a mantel shelf made by combining different styles of store-bought molding *(pages 104-105)*. You can also order a full mantel from a specialty company, or have one fashioned by a cabinetmaker.

 TOOLS

Tape measure	Sanding block	Tile cutter
Miter box	Brick set	Notched trowel
and backsaw	Ball-peen	Rubber-faced
Hammer	hammer	float
Nail set	Mason's trowel	C-clamps
	Nylon straps	Screwdriver
	Rubber mallet	Putty knife

MATERIALS

	Portland cement	Crown molding
Bricks	Slate or marble	Half-round
Fireplace mortar	hearthstone	molding ($\frac{1}{2}$")
Floorboards	Ceramic tiles	Lumber
Molding	Latex-Portland	($1\frac{1}{2}$" thick)
Finishing nails	cement tile mortar	Wood strip
($1\frac{1}{2}$", 2")	Cement-based	($\frac{1}{2}$" thick)
Carpenter's glue	grout	2 x 2
Sandpaper	Dentil molding	Wood screws
Mason's sand	Baseboard	(3" No. 8)
	molding	Wood filler

SAFETY TIPS

Wear goggles when nailing and when cutting brick or tile. Put on gloves to work with fireplace mortar, and hard-toed shoes when laying a slate or marble hearthstone.

A SIMPLE BRICK HEARTH AND FACING

1. Laying the hearth.
◆ Arrange a dry run of bricks on the hearth slab, spacing the units $\frac{1}{2}$ inch apart. Cut bricks as needed.
◆ Spread a bed of fireplace mortar $\frac{1}{2}$ inch thick on the slab, then lay the bricks. When the mortar is thumbprint-hard, level the mortar joints so the hearth will be easier to clean.
◆ Cover the gap between the hearth and the surrounding floor with hardwood floorboards.

To cover the hearth slab with tiles or flagstones, first raise the level of the hearth slab with an additional layer of concrete so the finished hearth will be at the level of the firebox floor. Lay the tiles using the techniques on page 103.

2. Measuring the molding.

◆ Hold the molding against one side of the brick facing and mark it in line with the top corner *(right)*. Repeat on the other side.

◆ With a miter box and backsaw, cut the marked ends of the molding at a 45-degree angle.

◆ Measure and cut both ends of the top piece of molding the same way, this time adding $\frac{1}{8}$ inch at each end for fitting adjustments.

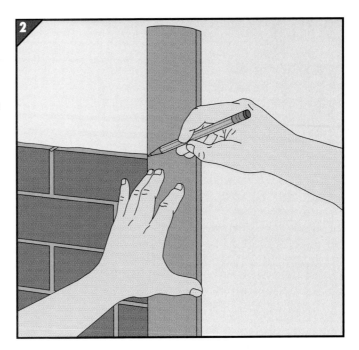

3. Fitting the miters.

◆ Attach the top piece of molding to the header above the fireplace with $1\frac{1}{2}$-inch finishing nails at 12-inch intervals, driving them only partway in.

◆ Butt one of the side pieces against the top molding and nail it to the wall the same way. Repeat for the opposite side molding.

◆ Finish driving in the nails and set them with a nail set. Lock each joint by driving a nail through the upper edge of the top molding into the end grain of a side piece *(left)*.

◆ Sand the joints smooth and apply a finish to the wood.

TRICKS OF THE TRADE

Fine-Tuning a Miter Joint

To make mitered joints fit perfectly, cut the pieces in a miter box, then tack them in place temporarily by driving the finishing nails halfway. Protect the surfaces behind the joint with cardboard, then saw through the corner with a dovetail saw, creating two parallel cuts *(right)*. Squeeze some carpenter's glue into the joint. Tap the pieces together to close the gap, then hammer in the nails.

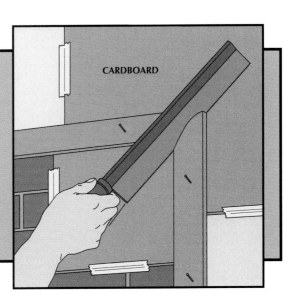

CARDBOARD

SETTING IN A SLATE OR MARBLE HEARTH

1. Positioning the hearth.

◆ Blend 3 parts sand with 1 part Portland cement and spread enough of the mixture on the hearth slab as a setting bed so the hearth will sit $\frac{1}{16}$ inch above the firebox floor.

◆ With a helper, loop two 2-inch-wide nylon straps around the hearthstone and lower it onto the setting bed *(right)*. Check the height of the stone and add or remove sand and cement as necessary.

◆ Lift the hearth from the bed and sprinkle a $\frac{1}{16}$-inch layer of dry cement over the setting bed. Mist the surface of the bed so it is damp, but not wet.

◆ Reposition the stone on the bed and pull out the straps.

◆ Push the hearth against the front edge of the firebox, centering it between the sides of the hearth slab.

SETTING BED

2. Leveling the slab.

◆ With a rubber mallet, tap the hearth down, working from one edge to the other. Periodically lay a long and straight board across the hearth and firebox, and continue tapping the hearth until its top surface is level with the firebox floor *(left)*.

◆ Cover the space between the hearth and the surrounding floor with hardwood floorboards, leaving a $\frac{1}{16}$-inch gap.

VENEERING THE FACE WITH TILE

1. Cementing the tiles.

◆ Plan the arrangement of the tiles so a joint will fall at the level of the top of the firebox. Mark the bottom row for cutting, if necessary. Tiles can overlap the wallboard around the fireplace by up to one-third their width.

◆ Trim the tiles with a tile cutter.

◆ Mix a batch of latex-Portland cement tile mortar and, with a notched trowel, spread a layer on the facing to one side of the firebox.

◆ Set the bottom row of tiles flush with the hearth, pressing the tiles into the cement.

◆ Continue laying tiles until the facing is entirely covered *(right)*.

◆ Let the cement cure for an hour, then clean the cement from the joints and sponge the tile surfaces with soap and water.

NOTCHED TROWEL

2. Grouting the joints.

◆ Prepare a batch of cement-based grout and spread it over the tiles with a rubber-faced float held on edge *(left)*. Force the grout into the joints by sweeping the float diagonally across the tiles, first in one direction then the other.

◆ Wait 10 minutes, then wipe off excess grout with a damp sponge—rinsing the sponge often in a pail of water—until the tile surfaces are clear. Do not rinse the sponge over a drain; the grout may clog it.

◆ When the grout is dry, polish the tiles with a soft, lint-free cloth.

◆ Frame the fireplace with wood molding *(page 101)* or leave it unframed.

A MANTEL SHELF SUPPORTED BY MOLDINGS

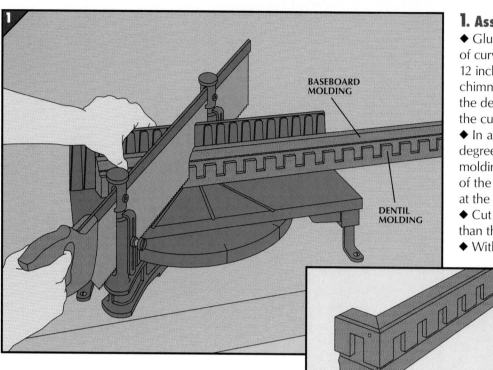

1. Assembling the shelf support.

◆ Glue dentil molding to the flat face of curved baseboard molding about 12 inches longer than the width of the chimney breast, aligning the teeth of the dentil molding along the edge of the curve on the baseboard molding.
◆ In a miter box adjusted for a 45-degree angle cut, saw two pieces of molding $2\frac{3}{4}$ inches long for the sides of the shelf support. Make each cut at the edge of a dentil tooth *(left)*.
◆ Cut the front piece 5 inches wider than the width of the chimney breast.
◆ With glue and $1\frac{1}{2}$-inch finishing nails, fasten the side pieces to the front piece, forming a three-sided box *(inset)*.

2. Adding crown molding.

◆ Set a length of crown molding in a miter box with its bottom edge against the fence. Miter one end at 45 degrees *(right)*.
◆ Miter the other end so the length of the molding along its bottom edge equals the length of the shelf support. Cut two side pieces from the crown molding waste to fit the support.
◆ Glue and clamp the crown molding to the dentil and baseboard molding so the bottom edge of the crown is flush with the top of the dentil teeth.
◆ For the shelf, cut a $1\frac{1}{2}$-inch-thick board 7 inches wide and 8 inches longer than the chimney breast width.
◆ Trim the front and sides of the shelf with $\frac{1}{2}$-inch half-round molding, mitered at the corners. Glue and clamp the molding to the edges of the shelf.
◆ With the shelf upside down on a table, align the back of the shelf flush with the back of the support and toenail the crown molding to the underside of the shelf with $1\frac{1}{2}$-inch finishing nails.

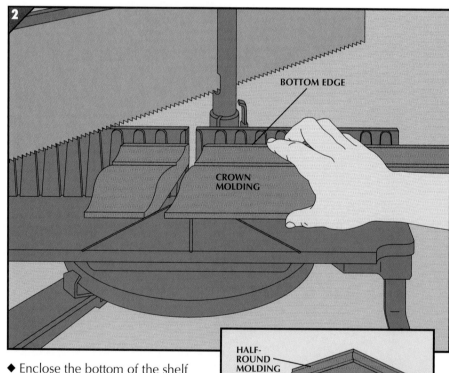

◆ Enclose the bottom of the shelf support with a $\frac{1}{2}$-inch-thick wood strip, cut to the inside dimensions of the box. Position the strip flush with the bottom of the box and nail through the baseboard molding to fasten it in place *(inset)*.

CLEAT

3. Mounting the shelf.
◆ Cut a 2-by-2 cleat 8 inches shorter than the interior dimensions of the box.
◆ With 3-inch No. 8 wood screws, fasten the cleat to the header above the chimney breast, lining up the bottom of the cleat 2 inches above the top of the brick facing.
◆ With a helper, set the shelf on the cleat, centering it over the chimney breast.
◆ Fasten the shelf to the cleat with 2-inch finishing nails spaced 4 inches apart *(left)*.
◆ Set the nails and fill the holes with wood filler.

A FULL FIREPLACE SURROUND

Made from hardwoods like oak, cherry, or walnut, a full surround can transform a fireplace into the focal point of a room *(right)*. You can commission a cabinetmaker to build one, but a more economical option is to buy a kit.

The minimum distance between the surround and the firebox is usually specified by local fire codes. It ranges from $3\frac{1}{2}$ to 7 inches along the sides and is typically at least 12 inches for a mantel shelf that overhangs the fireplace opening by more than

$1\frac{1}{2}$ inches. The inner edges of the surround lie on the brick facing; its outer edges extend onto the wallboard and are nailed to studs on each side of the fireplace.

The margin of brick between the surround and the fireplace opening can be left exposed, or covered with a three-piece stone-veneer frame.

The Care and Feeding of a Fire

Keeping a home heated with a fireplace or wood stove takes a bit of work. But the tasks involved are actually not as difficult or as time-consuming as you might think. From felling a tree and splitting logs to kindling a fire or cleaning a flue, your job will be easier if you have the right knowledge and the right tools.

Splitting a log for firewood →

A Recipe for a Perfect Fire

There is no great mystery to building and maintaining a hearty fire. All it takes is some good dry wood *(pages 116-117)* and a basic understanding of what makes a fire catch and keep going.

Preparing for the Fire: Properly laid wood and kindling are key to starting and maintaining a fire *(opposite and page 110)*. Once you have the fuel in place, you can kick-start the draft: In a fireplace, open the damper and hold a burning torch made from a rolled-up newspaper directly under the damper. For a wood stove, burn a couple of sheets of newspaper in the firebox. The warmed air will rise, pulling fresh air into the stove. If the fuel is well arranged, a single match will ignite the paper and kindling, and the heat of the fire will sustain the draft.

Nurturing the Blaze: A fire needs enough air for full combustion, but not so much that it drives the flames too hard or pulls excess air up the flue. Once the kindling is burning well or is reduced to embers, load logs into the firebox for a long burn. On a wood stove, leave the door ajar for the first few minutes after the fire catches, then control the airflow by opening or closing the vents as needed. With a fireplace, adjust the damper to control the draft. It may take some practice to find the right balance, but in either case, too much air is better than too little.

 TOOLS

Metal ash can	Tongs
Fire bellows	Fireplace shovel
Poker	and brush

 **MATERIALS**

Newspaper	Firewood
Kindling	Matches

 SAFETY TIPS

Wear fireproof gloves when tending to a fire.

Tools for tending an open fire.

This fireplace is equipped with the basic accessories required to keep fires safely contained and make them easy to manage. The wide iron grate supports the fuel and allows air to circulate around and under the fire. The fire screen keeps burning embers inside the firebox. A good set of fire tools includes a metal can with a tight-fitting lid to collect ashes for disposal outdoors; fireproof gloves to protect your hands while you tend a fire; bellows to fan dying embers or increase airflow during kindling; a poker at least 28 inches long for stirring up a fire and spreading out embers; tongs for moving and turning logs; a shovel to collect ashes or hot coals; a brush for sweeping up ashes; and a basket for storing extra wood near the fireplace.

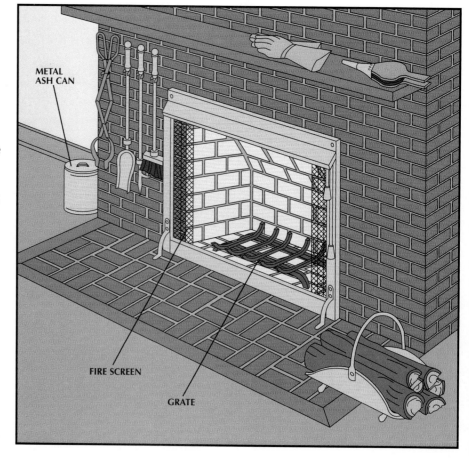

METAL ASH CAN

FIRE SCREEN

GRATE

Lighting a fire.

◆ Lay a bed of four or five sheets of crumpled newspaper.
◆ Set several layers of finger-thick kindling on top of the newspaper.
◆ Place a few larger pieces of kindling on top of the pile.
◆ Light the paper with a match *(left)*.
◆ When the kindling is burning well, or when only charcoal and embers remain, load firewood into the stove or fireplace *(page 110)*.

TRICKS OF THE TRADE

A Fire That Burns from the Top Down

In many modern wood stoves, reversing the fire-building method described above by laying the large logs first and following with kindling and paper can have several benefits. First, you can place larger logs in the firebox right away, without waiting for a fire to become well established. Second, fires built this way tend to produce less smoke. This technique works best in advanced-combustion stoves, in which there is sufficient air turbulence in the firebox to move air across the fuel. In older stoves with only simple air inlets at the bottom, the direction of the draft will prevent this method from working well.

LOADING A FIREBOX

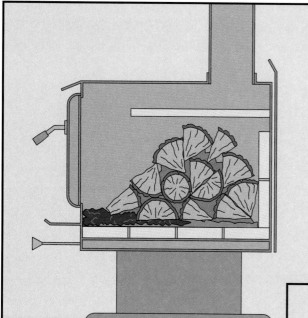

Loading logs for a long burn.
◆ Rake the charcoal and embers toward the front of the stove or fireplace.
◆ Pile dry logs in the firebox, filling it about two-thirds full, as shown at left. If the kindling is still burning, the firewood can be placed perpendicular to the opening instead of parallel.
◆ Open all the inlets and let the fire burn for 15 to 30 minutes, or until all the wood is charred.
◆ Decrease the airflow into the firebox to slow the rate of burning, but do not cut off so much air that the fire starts smoldering.

Creating a flash fire.
A loosely laid fire will burn up quickly, generating enough heat to quickly warm a chilly room.
◆ If the kindling is reduced to charcoal and embers, rake them forward.
◆ Lay four or five logs in a crisscross pattern *(right)*.
◆ Leave all the inlets open until most of the wood is burned. You can contain the fire slightly by restricting the airflow, but do not allow the flames to go out.
◆ When there is nothing left but charcoal, load the stove for a long burn as described above.

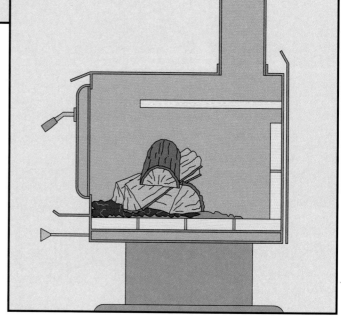

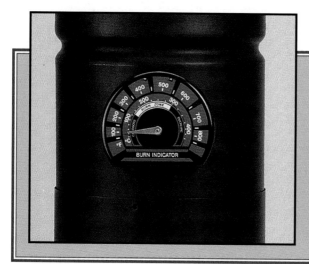

KEEPING TABS ON THE FLUE

Maintaining a steady temperature is the most efficient way to heat a house. You can monitor a heater's temperature with a flue-mounted thermometer *(left)*: Keep it between 300° and 550° F—if it is too cold, add fuel or air; if it is too hot, cut back on the air supply. Creosote buildup in the flue will also be minimized, since this temperature range prevents gases from condensing as they rise.

Keeping the Flue Clean

When a fire burns, residues in the form of soot and creosote are deposited inside the flue. These substances—both of which are flammable—are a major cause of chimney fires. Regular cleaning is crucial in eliminating the deposits.

Inspecting the Flue: Though the average chimney needs sweeping only once every two years, the flue of a fireplace that gets heavy and continuous use, or of a stove that is airtight, may need cleaning much more often. A monthly inspection is a good idea, at least until you become familiar with the rate at which your stove or fireplace collects deposits. When the buildup is more than $\frac{1}{8}$ inch thick, the flue needs cleaning, as well as the smoke chamber of a fireplace.

Sweeping the Chimney: Fireplace chimneys can be swept from inside the house *(below and page 112)*, while vertical metal flues can be cleaned only from above *(pages 114-115)*. Cleaning tools are available at fireplace supply stores. For the chimney brush to work well, get one that matches the flue's inside dimensions. If you have to work on the roof, observe the safety measures outlined on page 18.

TOOLS

Wrench	Steel flue scraper
Pliers	Long-handled pot brush
Utility knife	Dustpan
Screwdriver	Weighted flue brush with rope
Flue brush with flexible rods	

MATERIALS

Polyethylene sheeting	Heavy plastic garbage bags
Duct tape	Newspaper
	Large paper bags

SAFETY TIPS

Wear goggles, gloves, and a dust mask when removing the damper or inspecting the flue.

SWEEPING A MASONRY CHIMNEY FROM BELOW

1. Accessing the flue.
◆ Remove the damper plate *(page 14)* by detaching the handle from the plate and tilting the plate out of the frame *(right)*. If a cotter pin anchors the lever to the plate, remove it and lift the plate from the frame. If the plate cannot be removed, swing it open as wide as possible and determine if there is enough room for the sweeping brush. If not, you will have to clean the chimney from the top or have a professional do the job.
◆ Look inside the smoke chamber—wearing goggles or using a mirror—to establish the size and shape of the flue, and obtain a flue brush of appropriate size.

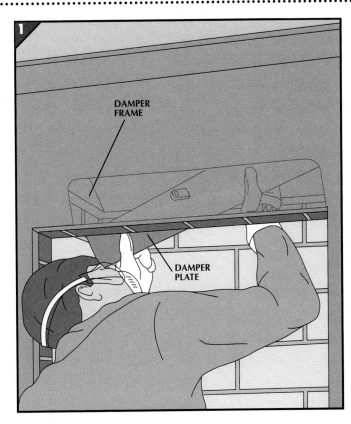

DAMPER FRAME

DAMPER PLATE

2. Sealing the fireplace opening.

◆ Cut a piece of polyethylene sheeting slightly larger than the fireplace opening. Seal it against the fireplace with continuous strips of duct tape along its top, bottom, and sides *(right)*.

◆ With a utility knife, make an inverted T-shaped cut 15 inches wide and 10 inches high in the center of the plastic. Watch the flaps created by the cut— they should be pulled into the fireplace, indicating the presence of an updraft that will carry loosened soot up and out the flue. If there is no updraft, create one by closing off the room, opening a window, and pulling air into the room with a fan.

◆ Cover the area in front of the hearth with newspaper or a drop cloth.

3. Sweeping the flue.

◆ Attach one rod section to the flue brush *(photograph)*, then slip the brush through the opening in the plastic, past the damper, and into the flue *(left)*.

◆ Work the brush up and down until the noise of falling debris subsides.

◆ Attach another section of rod to the bottom of the first and push the brush up to clean the next section of flue.

◆ Continue adding rods and sweeping the flue until the brush reaches the top of the flue.

◆ Pull the brush down to the smoke chamber and detach all but the first rod section.

4. Cleaning the smoke chamber.

◆ Scrub the walls of the smoke chamber vigorously, first with the flue brush then with a pot brush *(left)*, to loosen deposits from the surface.

◆ Slip a large doubled paper bag through the opening in the plastic. Holding the bag open with one hand, sweep in debris from the smoke shelf. With a dustpan, remove debris from the firebox floor.

◆ Inspect the flue for glazed creosote; if there is any, remove it *(page 114)*.

TRICKS OF THE TRADE

A Shop-Made Flue Brush

A brush designed like the one at right can effectively scour a flue from above. Cut a 4-inch-wide block to length so a wire brush attached to each end will make the assembly $\frac{1}{2}$ inch wider than the flue width. To assemble the unit, drill two 1-inch-diameter holes into the top edge of the block and glue a 1-inch dowel into each hole. To make a handle, fasten a third dowel to the first two with hose clamps. Pull bristles from a hole near the center of each wire brush and drill pilot holes through this hole and into the block; secure the brushes to the block with 2-inch No. 8 screws, and clamp the top ends of the brushes to the dowels. Extend the flue brush by clamping additional lengths of dowel to the handle.

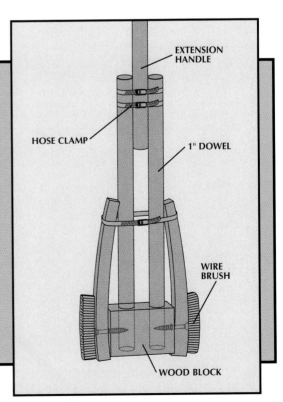

EXTENSION HANDLE

HOSE CLAMP

1" DOWEL

WIRE BRUSH

WOOD BLOCK

REMOVING A COATING OF GLAZED CREOSOTE

Scraping the creosote.
◆ Attach the steel flue scraper to a rod section and slip it through the plastic sheet, up into the flue. Add rod sections to extend the scraper to the top of the flue.
◆ Scrape the flue with an up-and-down motion, rolling your wrists clockwise on the upstroke, then pulling the scraper straight down *(right)*.
◆ Once the noise of falling debris subsides, detach a rod section and work on the next section. Work your way down the flue, scraping until you reach the bottom.

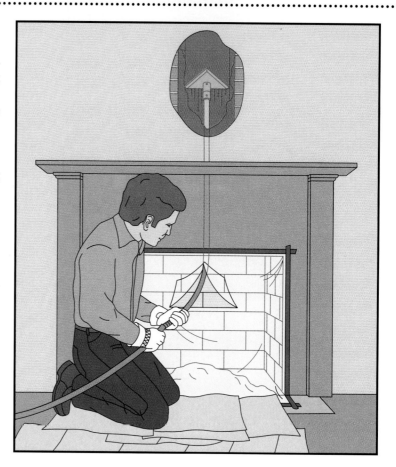

CLEARING A VERTICAL FLUE

1. Opening the flue.
◆ Spread newspapers on the floor under the flue pipe.
◆ For a stove with a flue collar at the back, remove any screws securing the pipe to the appliance and pull it off *(left)*; detach the elbow. If the collar is on top of the stove, unless you have a telescoping section *(page 41, photograph)*, remove any screws holding the pipe to the collar and to the chimney-pipe support at the ceiling; detach the bottom section of pipe. Push up the upper part of the pipe enough to allow you to remove the bottom section, then lower it and have a helper reattach it at the chimney-pipe support.
◆ With duct tape, fasten a large double-thick paper or plastic bag to the open end of the pipe to catch debris.

2. Sweeping the flue.

◆ Observing the precautions for safety at heights *(page 18)*, climb to the roof and remove the chimney cap. If the stovepipe extends too high above the roof for you to work comfortably, remove a section of pipe.

◆ Lower a weighted brush *(right)*, or a brush extended by rods, to the bottom of the flue. Have a helper inside warn you just before the brush reaches the catch bag.

◆ Pull the brush up the flue gradually, using up-and-down strokes as you go.

◆ When you have finished sweeping the main portion of the flue, take the dismantled elbow or pipe segment outside and clean it.

◆ Carefully remove the catch bag and reassemble the flue.

◆ Clean the interior of the firebox with a pot brush.

WEIGHT

CLEANING A HORIZONTAL PIPE

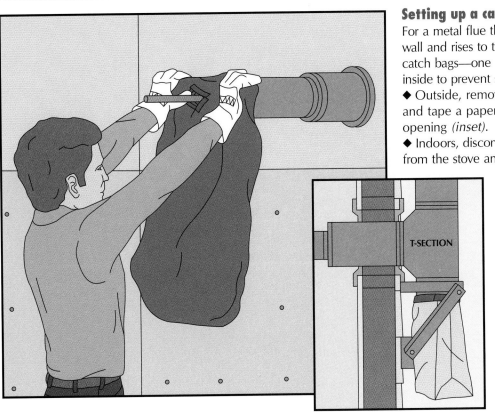

T-SECTION

Setting up a catch-bag system.

For a metal flue that passes through an exterior wall and rises to the roof outside, you'll need two catch bags—one outside to collect debris, and one inside to prevent soot from entering the house.

◆ Outside, remove the cap from the T-section and tape a paper or plastic bag around the opening *(inset)*.

◆ Indoors, disconnect the vertical pipe and elbow from the stove and horizontal pipe *(opposite, Step 1)*; clean them outside.

◆ Insert a flue brush and one section of rod in the horizontal pipe.

◆ Cut a slit for the rod through a heavy plastic garbage bag, reinforce the slit with duct tape, and tape the bag to the pipe *(left)*.

◆ Working slowly, push the brush back and forth, directing the debris into the outside catch bag. When you're finished, slide the brush into the garbage bag before untaping it from the pipe.

Buying, Storing, and Chopping Firewood

Firewood is measured by the cord—a term denoting a stack 8 feet long, 4 feet high, and 4 feet wide. Dealers usually sell dry firewood in partial cords called face cords, which are the length and height of a full cord, but only as wide as the logs are long, usually 16 inches.

Selecting Wood: The best wood species for firewood are dense woods such as maple, but any species can be used as fuel *(opposite)*. Seasoned—or dry—logs are sold split and ready to burn. To test wood for dryness, toss two logs into the air so they collide. Dry logs make a sharp, ringing sound; you will hear a dull thud if the wood is green—or contains too much moisture.

Unseasoned Wood: Green wood costs less than seasoned, but it is made up of about one-half water. It will smolder when lit, producing a good deal of smoke and little flame. Much of the fire's heat is wasted evaporating the water. Burning unseasoned wood will also cause a rapid buildup of creosote in the flue. You will have to split the logs yourself, and let them dry for several months before they can be burned. Wood that is cut, split, and stacked properly in early spring should be ready by fall. Wet wood should be stacked in a sunny spot that is exposed to the wind *(below)*. Keep the logs off the ground so air can circulate under them, preventing rot. Once the wood is seasoned, a small supply can be stored at the ready in a shed *(opposite)*.

 TOOLS

Circular saw
Hammer
Screwdriver

Splitting wedges
Sledgehammer
  (6 to 12 pound)
Splitting maul

 **MATERIALS**

Concrete blocks
Pressure-treated wood
  (2 x 2s, 2 x 4s,
  2 x 8s, 2 x 10s)
Exterior-grade
  plywood ($\frac{3}{4}$")

Galvanized common nails ($3\frac{1}{2}$")
Galvanized
  wood screws
  (2" No. 8)
Plastic sheeting
Splitting stump

 SAFETY TIPS

Wear eye protection when striking a wedge with a sledgehammer, and put on hard-toed shoes or boots to protect your feet from dropped logs.

Stacking and seasoning firewood.
◆ Lay three rows of concrete blocks over an area about 10 feet long and 8 feet wide.
◆ Set a 2-by-10 on each row of blocks.
◆ Drive a 2-by-4 support 1 foot into the ground at each end of the 2-by-10s.
◆ Brace the supports with diagonal 2-by-4s beveled at the top end. Fasten the diagonal boards at the top with $3\frac{1}{2}$-inch galvanized common nails. At ground level, hold them in place with 2-by-2 stakes.
◆ Pile the logs on the 2-by-10s with at least 12 inches between rows to allow air to circulate.
◆ Cover the top of each stack with a sheet of plastic, held down with logs.

A shed for keeping wood dry.

◆ Cut two pieces of $\frac{3}{4}$-inch plywood to the desired dimensions of the shed's sides, angling the top edge downward for the roof slope.

◆ With 2-inch No. 8 galvanized wood screws, fasten each piece of plywood to 2-by-4s cut to fit around its edges, with the vertical boards extending beyond the bottom of the plywood as legs for the shed.

◆ Cut a third piece of plywood for the back of the shed and fasten it to each side piece, enlisting a helper to hold the parts steady.

◆ Leaving an overhang at the front, cut a last piece of plywood for the roof and screw it to the frame.

◆ Nail 2-by-8s across the lower 2-by-4s for the floor, and cover the shed with roofing and siding materials.

GETTING THE MOST HEAT VALUE FOR YOUR MONEY

Heat Value Per Cord	Wood Species	Splitting and Burning Characteristics
High: 24-30 million BTUs	Hickory (hardwood)	Moderately hard to split; moderately hard to ignite; makes long-lasting charcoal
	Beech (hardwood)	Hard to split; hard to ignite; burns fairly well unseasoned
	Sugar maple (hardwood)	Moderately hard to split; hard to ignite; fragrant
	Oak (hardwood)	Moderately hard to split; hard to ignite; makes long-lasting charcoal
	Ash (hardwood)	Moderately easy to split; moderately hard to ignite; burns fairly well unseasoned
Medium: 16-23 million BTUs	Elm (hardwood)	Very hard to split; moderately hard to ignite; produces moderate amount of smoke
	Gum (hardwood)	Hard to split; moderately hard to ignite; produces moderate amount of smoke
	Sycamore (hardwood)	Hard to split; moderately hard to ignite; produces moderate amount of smoke
	Red maple (hardwood)	Easy to split; moderately hard to ignite; makes long-lasting charcoal
	Douglas fir (softwood)	Easy to split; easy to ignite; produces heavy amounts of smoke and sparks
Low: 13-15 million BTUs	Poplar (hardwood)	Easy to split; moderately hard to ignite; burns quickly; produces heavy amount of sparks
	Spruce (softwood)	Easy to split; easy to ignite; produces heavy amount of sparks
	Aspen (hardwood)	Easy to split; easy to ignite; produces moderate amount of smoke and heavy amount of sparks

Although all wood species have about the same energy content per pound, they vary in density. The hardwoods and softwoods above are listed in descending order according to their heat value per cord, measured in BTUs (British thermal units). Other characteristics worth considering—such as how difficult the wood is to split or how long its coals last—are listed at the right.

1. Starting the wedge.

◆ Set the log, large end up, on a splitting stump that is about 1 foot high, and wider than it is tall.

◆ Hold a steel splitting wedge against the log between the center and the edge, perpendicular to the wood grain; if there is an open crack radiating from the center of the log, insert the wedge into it. Alternatively, use a twisted wedge *(photograph)*, which splits wood more easily and is less likely to get stuck.

◆ With a 6- to 12-pound long-handled sledgehammer, tap the wedge into the wood deep enough for it to stand on its own *(right)*.

2. Driving the wedge.

Holding the sledgehammer with both hands, pound the wedge down, gradually splitting the log *(left)*. Swing the hammer only as high as you feel comfortable, and do not force the sledge downward—let it fall onto the wedge, allowing gravity to do most of the work. With practice, you will be able to execute a full, overhead swing of the hammer and hit the wedge squarely.

For an especially large or hard-to-split log, repeat the procedure with a second wedge, working in a line across the center of the log until it splits.

For logs up to 6 inches in diameter, you can try a splitting maul *(photograph)* which is designed to split logs in one blow. It works best with straight-grained wood.

SOLVING SPECIAL PROBLEMS

Freeing a stuck wedge.
When a wedge gets jammed in the end of a log, tap a second wedge into the wood between the stuck wedge and the center of the log *(right)*. Open a crack wide enough to release the first wedge.

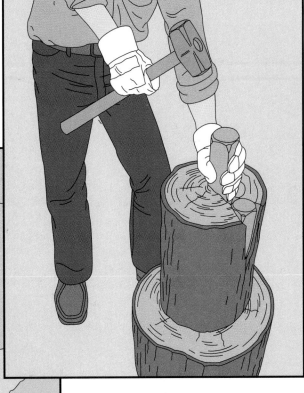

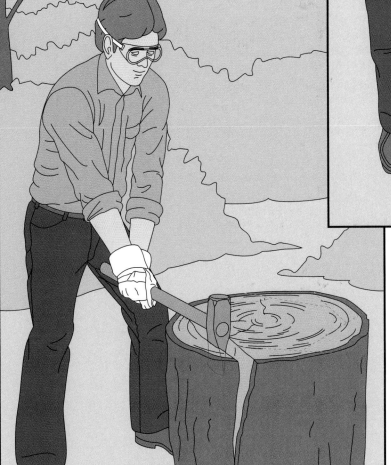

Whittling down a thick log.
A log more than 18 inches in diameter may be difficult to split with one or two blows.
◆ Hold a splitting maul parallel to the wood grain and strike the log 4 to 6 inches from its perimeter, splitting a wedge of wood from the log *(left)*. A wedge and a sledgehammer can be used instead.
◆ Work around the log until the core that remains is small enough to split as shown opposite.

A MACHINE TO LIGHTEN THE TASK

A power splitter like the one at right uses a hydraulic ram to force a wedge through a log; the wood is placed on the base and a lever activates the ram. Other models push the log through a stationary wedge. The splitter makes quick work of even difficult jobs such as logs longer than 16 inches or wood with twisty grain and knots.

Harvesting Trees Safely and Efficiently

If you have a few extra acres, harvesting firewood from your own trees can be an economical and rewarding alternative to obtaining it from a woodlot.

Operating a Chain Saw: Although electric chain saws are available for light duty, most people choose a gasoline-and-oil-powered chain saw *(below)*, with which a tree can be felled in minutes. The saw also simplifies two follow-up jobs: trimming off limbs and cutting the trunk into logs of suitable length for a fireplace or stove—a process called bucking a tree *(page 124)*. Choose a saw that is powerful enough for the job, but light enough to handle all day; and learn how it works. Keep the teeth well sharpened and check the fuel before starting; running out of gas halfway through a felling cut is dangerous.

Felling a Tree: Until you are experienced at felling trees, it is best to restrict your efforts to trees whose

diameter is less than the length of your saw's guide bar. Even with a small tree, it's difficult to predict exactly how and where it will fall once the cuts have been made. In planning the fall, consider the tree's natural lean, the concentration of its branches, and the wind direction. Although it's easiest to fell a tree toward its natural lean, it may not always be possible; another tree may be in the way, or the fall may be across a power line. With wedges and a special tapered cut called a hinge *(page 122)*, you may be able to direct a tree 90 degrees away from its natural lean, provided the lean is not too severe. If it is, a block and tackle can be used to guide the tree as it falls *(page 123)*.

Avoid felling trees on steep slopes; limbing and bucking are difficult and dangerous in such locations. Before you begin cutting, clear the area of people and make sure you have an escape route away from any possible line of fall.

 TOOLS

Chain saw
Sawhorse
Wooden wedges
Sledgehammer
Pulley

 **MATERIALS**

Hold-down strap
Nylon rope ($\frac{5}{8}$" dia.)

 SAFETY TIPS

Wear a hard hat, hearing protection, goggles or a face shield, work gloves, and steel-toed boots when operating a chain saw.

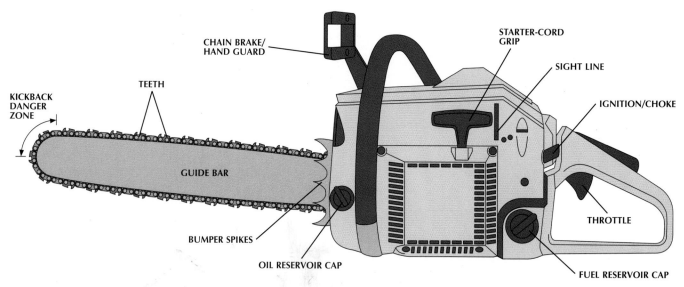

Anatomy of a chain saw.

Small teeth on a chain linked around a guide bar provide the cutting action of a chain saw. The operator holds the tool by the front handle to position it, and by the rear grip to push the guide bar into the cut. Bumper spikes stabilize the machine against the wood. When the saw is used to fell a tree, the sight line—a mark on the engine housing—points in the direction the tree will fall. In the event of a kickback *(opposite)*, the chain-brake lever—an essential safety feature—hits the operator's hand and stops the chain. The lever also acts as a shield should the chain break.

Saws powered by gasoline and oil *(above)* are started with an ignition and a pull cord, with a choke used on a cold engine. The chain's speed is controlled by a trigger throttle.

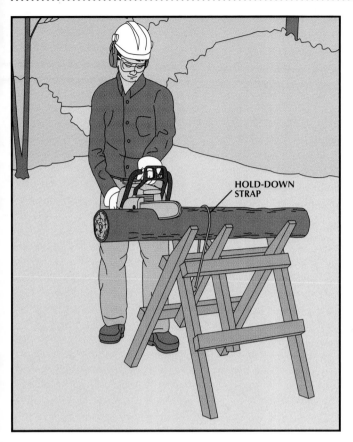

Techniques for safe cutting.

Try to position yourself to one side of the blade—should the saw kick back or cut through wood more quickly than expected, it will not hit you. When cutting lightweight logs to stovebox length, set them in a log-cutting sawhorse, attaching the hold-down strap to keep the log from moving *(left)*.

Avoiding kickback.

Most chain saw accidents result from kickback: When the upper part of the guide-bar tip—known as the kickback danger zone—contacts any solid object, the guide bar will jump back toward the operator *(right)*.

Although some chain saws have safety features to prevent kickback, handling the saw correctly is the best insurance. Always be aware of the guide-bar tip's location, and never cut with the tip. Watch for objects behind the one you are cutting; such hazards may be obscured by branches or leaves.

CHAIN-SAW SAFETY CLOTHING

If you plan to do a lot of log-cutting, consider special safety clothing *(photograph)*. The leg coverings, or "chaps," as well as the gloves and boots, are lined with a protective material, and the helmet includes ear and eye protection.

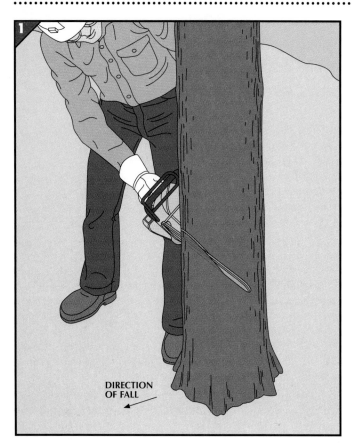

DIRECTION OF FALL

1. Starting a notch with an angled cut.
◆ Aligning the sight line with the fall direction, hold the guide bar at an angle of about 45 degrees to the trunk.
◆ Bring the engine to full throttle and ease the guide bar into the tree.
◆ Cut one-fifth to one-quarter of the way through the trunk *(left)*.
◆ Reduce the engine speed and remove the guide bar from the cut.

2. Finishing the notch.
◆ Hold the guide bar horizontally at the bottom of the angled cut.
◆ Keeping the sight line aimed toward the fall direction, make a horizontal cut that meets the end of the first one *(right)*.
◆ Pull out the guide bar and push the wedge-shaped waste piece from the notch.

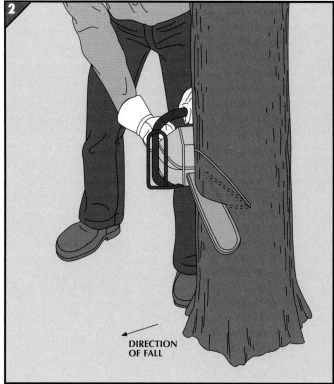

DIRECTION OF FALL

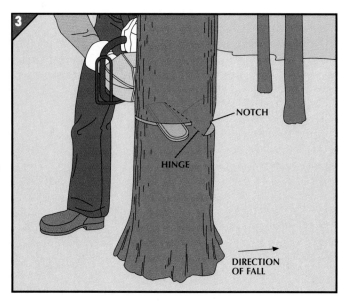

NOTCH

HINGE

DIRECTION OF FALL

3. Making the felling cut.
◆ On the side of the tree directly opposite the notch, make a horizontal cut 1 to 2 inches above the bottom of the notch *(left)*. End the cut about 2 inches short of the back of the notch, creating a hinge. The trunk will pivot on the hinge, causing the tree to fall. The instant the tree begins to move, release the throttle, withdraw the guide bar, switch off the saw, and retreat at a 45-degree angle from the fall direction.
◆ If the tree doesn't fall or leans back, pinching the blade, force it over with wedges *(opposite, Step 2)*.

DIRECTING THE FALL OF A SMALL TREE

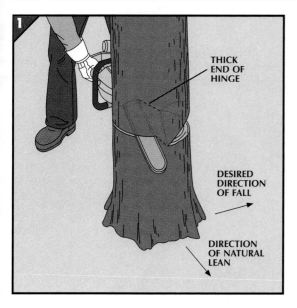

1. Cutting an angled hinge.
To make a tree fall away from its natural lean, cut a notch (opposite, Steps 1 and 2) on the side of the tree facing the desired direction of fall. Then make the felling cut opposite the notch (opposite, Step 3), but swivel the guide bar so the hinge will be thicker at the end opposite the direction of lean. When the tree falls, the wider end of the hinge should pull the tree in the desired direction.

◆ If the tree begins to fall as you finish the felling cut, withdraw the guide bar, cut the engine, and retreat at a 45-degree angle from the fall direction. If the tree remains standing, use wedges to encourage it to fall (Step 2).

2. Driving wedges.
◆ At the narrow end of the hinge, drive two wooden wedges into the felling cut (right); plastic wedges are also available (photograph). The wedges will shift the tree's center of gravity toward the notch.
◆ If the tree doesn't fall, drive in larger wedges.

Wedges can also help release a stuck saw by bearing the weight of the tree that has settled back on the chain; but avoid touching the chain with the wedge.

GUIDING A FALL WITH BLOCK AND TACKLE

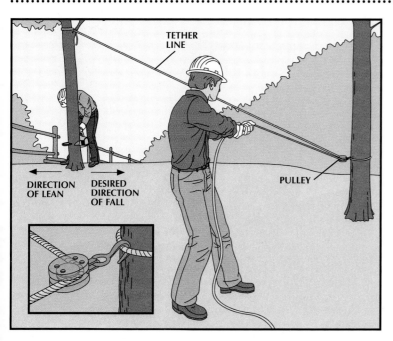

Attaching a tether line and pulley.
◆ Tie a $\frac{5}{8}$-inch nylon-rope tether line around the tree to be felled, placing the rope as high on the trunk as you can reach. Run the line to another tree that is roughly in line with the desired direction of fall, and fasten a pulley assembly (inset) to its trunk about 2 feet from the ground.
◆ Feed the tether line through the pulley.
◆ Have a helper, standing at a 90-degree angle to the line formed by the two trees at a distance equal to at least twice the height of the tree to be felled, pull the line taut.
◆ Cut a notch in line with the desired direction of fall (opposite, Steps 1 and 2).
◆ As you are making the felling cut (opposite, Step 3), have your helper pull on the tether line to direct the fall (left).

TRIMMING LIMBS FROM A TRUNK

Limbing the tree.
◆ Starting at the top of the tree, hold the guide bar parallel to the trunk, keeping the trunk between you and the saw. Cut toward the bottom of the tree through the base of the limb *(right)*; don't let the tip of the guide bar hit the ground or any branches.

◆ Cut off all the limbs on one side, then move to the other side of the trunk and limb the opposite side. Leave the limbs on the underside of the trunk intact, to raise and support the trunk during bucking.

If the tree lies across a slight incline, brace the trunk by leaving several limbs on the downhill side to keep it from rolling. Stand on the uphill side to make the limbing cuts. Adjust your stance to keep your legs away from the guide bar when cutting limbs on the uphill side.

SAWING A TREE INTO MANAGEABLE LENGTHS

1. Beginning the bucking cut.
With the saw's guide bar under the tree and its bumper spikes against the trunk, pivot the bar up to cut through roughly one-third of the trunk *(left)*.

2. Finishing the cut.
◆ Rest the guide bar across the top of the trunk aligned with the first bucking cut.

◆ Using the bumper spikes as a fulcrum, pivot the guide bar down through the trunk to meet the first cut. Repeat the top cut from the opposite side of the trunk, if necessary.

◆ Once the trunk has been halved, roll each log onto one side and saw off any remaining limbs.

CUTTING IN DIFFICULT SITUATIONS

Bucking a tree flat on the ground.
◆ Make the first cut straight down, halfway through the trunk.
◆ Withdraw the guide bar from the trunk, turn the saw off, and tap a wedge into the top of the cut to keep the chain from binding.
◆ Restart the engine, and without pressing the throttle, slide the guide bar back into the cut. Then continue cutting downward, taking care to stop before the guide bar hits the ground *(right)*. The log should break apart on its own; if not, kick the log sharply to sever it.

For a slender trunk, make a top cut halfway through the trunk, then roll the trunk over, and cut down again to meet the first cut.

Cutting an unsupported section.
To prevent cut trunk sections from falling toward the guide bar and pinching it, make the first cut from the top through one-third of the trunk. Then cut up from the underside *(left)*. Be ready to withdraw should either log move toward you.

Making angled bucking cuts.
When a section of trunk is balanced in such a way that one cut section is likely to remain stationary while the other falls toward the guide bar, make the two bucking cuts at an angle to prevent binding.
◆ Make the first cut from the top, angling it downward toward the section of the tree that will remain stationary. Saw one-third of the way through the trunk *(right)*.
◆ To sever the pieces, cut up from underneath at about the same angle.

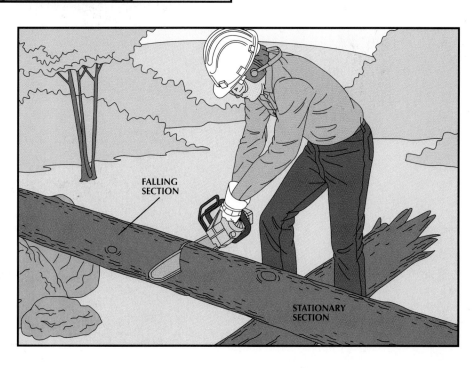

FALLING SECTION

STATIONARY SECTION

TIME® LIFE BOOKS

Time-Life Books is a division of Time Life Inc.

TIME LIFE INC.
PRESIDENT and CEO: George Artandi

TIME-LIFE BOOKS
PRESIDENT: John D. Hall
PUBLISHER/MANAGING EDITOR:
Neil Kagan

HOME REPAIR AND IMPROVEMENT:
Fireplaces and Wood Stoves
EDITOR: Lee Hassig
MARKETING DIRECTOR: James Gillespie
Deputy Editor: Esther R. Ferington
Art Director: Kathleen Mallow
Associate Editor/Research and Writing:
  Karen Sweet
Marketing Manager: Wells Spence

Vice President, Director of Finance:
  Christopher Hearing
Vice President, Book Production:
  Marjann Caldwell
Director of Operations: Eileen Bradley
Director of Photography and Research:
  John Conrad Weiser
Director of Editorial Administration:
  Judith W. Shanks
Production Manager: Marlene Zack
Quality Assurance Manager: James King
Library: Louise D. Forstall

ST. REMY MULTIMEDIA INC.
President and Chief Executive Officer:
  Fernand Lecoq
President and Chief Operating Officer:
  Pierre Léveillé
Vice President, Finance: Natalie Watanabe
Managing Editor: Carolyn Jackson
Managing Art Director: Diane Denoncourt
Production Manager: Michelle Turbide

Staff for *Fireplaces and Wood Stoves*

Series Editors: Marc Cassini, Heather Mills
Series Art Director: Francine Lemieux
Art Director: Robert Paquet
Assistant Editor: John Dowling
Designers: François Daxhelet,
  Jean-Guy Doiron, Robert Labelle
Editorial Assistant: James Piecowye
Coordinator: Dominique Gagné
Copy Editor: Judy Yelon
Indexer: Linda Cardella Cournoyer
Systems Coordinator: Éric Beaulieu
Other Staff: Linda Castle, Lorraine Doré,
  Geneviève Monette

PICTURE CREDITS
Cover: Photograph, Robert Chartier.
  Art, Robert Paquet. Wood stove provided by Pacific Energy Wood Stoves

Illustrators: Jack Arthur, Gilles Beauchemin,
  Frederic F. Bigio (B-C Graphics), Michel
  Blais, Roger Essley, Charles Forsythe,
  William J. Hennessy Jr., Elsie J. Hennig,
  Walter Hilmers Jr. (HJ Commercial Art),
  John Jones, Arezou Katoozian, Dick Lee,
  John Martinez, John Massey, Joan
  McGurren, Eduino J. Pereira (Arts &
  Words), Jacques Perrault

Photographers: **End papers:** Glenn Moores
  and Chantal Lamarre. **12:** First Alert Inc.
  **15, 18, 24, 41, 64, 75, 78, 110, 118,
  121, 123:** Glenn Moores and Chantal
  Lamarre. **29:** Reggio Register Co. **45:**
  Martin Industries. **58:** Stanley Tools.
  105: Collinswood Designs. **112:** Schaefer Brush Manufacturing Co., Inc. **119:**
  White by MTD.

ACKNOWLEDGMENTS
The editors wish to thank the following individuals and institutions: Ames/Garant, St-François, Quebec; Appalachian Stove & Fabricators, Inc., Asheville, NC; Collinswood Designs, Fort Collins, CO; Country Stoves Inc., Auburn, WA; Deer Hill Enterprises, Cummington, MA; Fireplace Technologies Inc., Louisville, KY; First Alert Inc., Aurora, IL; Louis V. Genuario, Genuario Construction Co., Inc. Alexandria, VA; GSW Heating Products Company, Worthington, OH; Guy Guenette Ltd., St-Laurent, Quebec; Hearth Products Association, Arlington, VA; Husqvarna Forest & Garden, Burnaby, British Columbia; Hy-C Company Inc., St. Louis, MO; Lambro Venting Products Inc., LaPrairie, Quebec; Martin Industries, Florence, AL; Natural Resources Canada, Energy Efficiency Branch, Ottawa, Ontario; Pacific Energy Wood Stoves (19860 Ltd.), Duncan, British Columbia; Quality-Flex, Waterloo, Ontario; R-Co Products Corp., Lakewood, NY; Reggio Register Co., Ayer, MA; Rutland Products, Rutland, VT; Schaefer Brush Manufacturing Co. Inc., Waukesha, WI; Stanley Tools, Div. of Stanley Works, New Britain, CT; Mark Steele, Mark Steele Associates Inc., Alexandria, VA; Stihl Limited, London, Ontario; White by MTD, Cleveland, OH

**Library of Congress
Cataloging-in-Publication Data**
Fireplaces and wood stoves / by the editors
  of Time-Life Books.
  p. cm. — (Home repair and improvement)
Includes index.
ISBN 0-7835-3907-X
1. Stoves, Wood. 2. Fireplaces
  I. Time-Life Books. II. Series.
TH7438.F5 1997
697'.1—dc21   96-37155